"I've seen the good, the bad, and the ugly when it comes to family reunions. Bob Wolfe's book on the *Secrets of Successful Family Reunions* is a great tool to help you make sure the generational values that have shaped your family are not lost in our high-tech, low-touch world."

- Rev. William Batson, MA
Founder/President
Family Builders
Cape Neddick, ME

"*Secrets of Successful Family Reunions* offers insightful observations about family reunions. Wolfe shares many lessons, triumphs, and discoveries."

- Edith Wagner
Editor
Reunions magazine

"What a great tool to help men like me move from good intention to good execution. What father and grandfather does not want to see his legacy continue and what better way to do this than through family reunions. *Secrets of Successful Family Reunions* gives multiple models to follow as we seek to build that legacy."

- Brian Doyle, National Director
Iron Sharpens Iron
West Hartford, CT

"Bob Wolfe's *Secrets of Successful Family Reunions* serves as a good model for writing the history of one's family reunion. Bob Wolfe has left a wonderful legacy for the family's future generations."

- Ione Dugger Vargus, Ph.D.
Founder and Chair, Family Reunion Institute
School of Social Administration , Temple University

"Bob's book takes family reunions to a new level, to a depth of relationship that very few families experience. Carving out that much time is a major challenge! Thanks to Bob and his family for setting a great example and for sharing their insights."

-Drew Crandall, President,
Northeast Christians At Work,
Vernon CT

"As a family member who has attended every reunion of our family from the first through the fortieth, I can attest to the fact that this book provides all the information needed to plan and carry out successful family reunions. After all these years, the fact that the young families look forward to and seem to be as interested in keeping it going as the older folks is proof of its success...For anyone interested in planning a family reunion with the hope of keeping it active and growing for a number of years, there is no better resource book anywhere than *Secrets of Successful Family Reunions* written by a man who has been instrumental in launching and keeping a family reunion going for forty years."

- Juanita Tryon—author's sister
Crown Point, IN

HELLO
my name is

Robert Wolfe
a.k.a. Uncle Bob

SECRETS OF SUCCESSFUL FAMILY REUNIONS

Have a *FABULOUS* Reunion
For Every Age—*Every Time*

Pass your values forward

TATE PUBLISHING *& Enterprises*

Secrets Of Sucessful Family Reunions
Copyright © 2008 by Robert W. Wolfe. All rights reserved.

This title is also available as a Tate Out Loud product. Visit www.tatepublishing.com for more information.

No part of this publication may be reproduced, stored in a retrieval system or transmitted in any way by any means, electronic, mechanical, photocopy, recording or otherwise without the prior permission of the author except as provided by USA copyright law.

The opinions expressed by the author are not necessarily those of Tate Publishing, LLC.

Published by Tate Publishing & Enterprises, LLC
127 E. Trade Center Terrace | Mustang, Oklahoma 73064 USA
1.888.361.9473 | www.tatepublishing.com

Tate Publishing is committed to excellence in the publishing industry. The company reflects the philosophy established by the founders, based on Psalm 68:11,
"The Lord gave the word and great was the company of those who published it."

Book design copyright © 2008 by Tate Publishing, LLC. All rights reserved.
Cover design by Nathan Harmony
Interior design by Kandi Evans

Published in the United States of America

ISBN: 978-1-60604-123-9
1. Family & Relationships
2. Cooking: Entertaining: Party Planning
08.03.17

Acknowledgements

I wish to express a debt of gratitude to my parents, Ora and Ann Wolfe, who in spite of the difficulties raising a family of seven children during the depression years of the late 1920s and '30s, instilled in us a tradition of love, belief, and support for one another.

I need to also acknowledge the support and contribution of my six siblings—Dale, Evah, James, Juanita, Max, and Ruth—in developing the family reunion from a casual event to a family tradition that has seemed to take on a life of its own. I would also be remiss if I did not recognize that this level of support would not have been possible without the involvement of their respective spouses, who were unusually tolerant of the Wolfe family idiosyncrasies.

I want to recognize my children—Linda, Karen, and Ken—who have offered both support and blunt critique that has been useful; and my extremely supportive wife, Ginnie, who offered encouragement and endlessly typed and retyped the manuscript.

In addition, a significant stimulus to writing this book was the many who have asked us, "How do you do it?" That became a real motivation to commit our methods to paper—a much bigger job than I expected.

I can only hope that other families will be encouraged and blessed by this book.

...the principles you will find in this book will build lasting memories for yourself and your family. My wife and five children all look forward to our annual family reunion. They have even commented, "Its the best weekend of the year."

- Stephen R. Phillips, CIC—author's nephew
W.J. Phillips, Inc.

"Weeks before we get to the Reunion, excitement builds as we plan our newest and best recipes to share, as well as outlining what we will say after our meals. Those yearly speeches as a young adult helped develop my skill as a workshop presenter and professional developer.....Build a reunion that can produce strong families of faith and memories that will truly last for generations to come."

- Mrs. Janice Kosiba—author's niece
Teacher and Professional Developer

"A successful family reunion renews the body, mind, and spirit and keeps a family's heritage alive. In today's culture, it is common for families to hire a wedding planner. Bob Wolfe could be considered America's Family Reunion Planner. His guidance to successful family reunions will be appreciated by families large or small."

-Michael W. Tryon—author's nephew
Business Owner,
State Representative
Crystal Lake, IL

"Have you ever tried to get family members together for a reunion? It's a struggle sometimes, but Uncle Bob started and kept a large, widely spread family meeting annually. These reunions have been happening for *forty years*! Bob's book will give tried and true strategies that will get your family started on a great tradition."

- Len Reichel—author's nephew
General Motor Executive

"Have you thought about planning a family reunion and don't know where to start? Would you like to form closer, more meaningful relationships with your extended family? For forty years our family has been doing just that, thanks to Uncle Bob. We meet annually to pass on family history and values, form relationships, and just have fun. Our own children have spread out around the country and make sure they plan vacation time for the 'Reunion'. It's a great way to stay connected in this fast-paced and crazy world!"

- Jean Wolfe—author's niece
Partner, Dale's Foods for Health
Flushing, MI

"Bob makes observations and gives insights on developing successful families and family relationships, not perfect, but successful families—a goal all our families would all benefit from."

- Rev. Dr. Karen L. Roy, Vernon, CT
Pastor, Grace Congregational Church,
Farmington, Connecticut

Secrets of Successful Family Reunions

CONTENTS

PREFACE

Why does my family feel so passionately about family reunions?
That thought fills my mind as I sit on my patio this
lovely fall afternoon, fresh from our fortieth annual family reunion. We had driven 1600 miles to be a part of the
sixty-two people who gathered to celebrate family in traditional fashion.

Our children drove even farther; even a grandchild flew
in to a nearby airport to attend this recent reunion so well
planned and completed by my sister's family, who was the
host family this year.

During World War II, our family—seven kids plus
mom and dad—was separated by necessity. Three of the
four brothers served their country, and two sisters married
men who also served. Feeling unusually blessed when all
returned, we reveled in the time we could spend together.

Perhaps my family, as a result of being caught in the
web of rapid industrial growth and moving eight times during the "family years," felt the need for the annual reunion
more strongly than those with more geographic stability.

Nevertheless, each family has been very supportive and
has contributed much to the plan presented in this book.

In addition to the sheer pleasure of being together, we
recognized that our children would grow up in a radically
different world than we had. We wanted to impart the same
work ethic, willingness to accept responsibility, values, and
faith that had been ingrained in us.

How to transmit these values was the question. Much

would need to be done within the individual nuclear family, but we knew wider family support would be helpful. We chose the family reunion as a way of building strong bonds, conveying family history, and instilling appreciation of our fore bearers who overcame significant difficulties without complaint.

INTRODUCTION

When our friends find that we have had forty years of family reunions with all generations enjoying and wishing to repeat them, a typical first question is, "What's your secret?"

As we try to explain this to others, we realize there is no one secret. However, we do not believe you will be disappointed; we are sharing the variety of attitudes, practices, programs, and activities that we have found successful.

Some were thoughtfully planned, some discovered by accident, and some just hit upon by luck. The sum total will let you know how one extended family, with simple lifestyles, has been inspired to continue to persevere year after year to a rewarding and fun-filled long weekend to keep the benefits of a family reunion alive.

Actually, when data was being gathered for this book, I visualized it as a Handbook for Family Reunions. This was intended to convey a specific message to the reader. Trained as an Engineer, I was taught that a handbook might be read once, but it's most important function is as a valuable permanent reference.

Through more than sixty years of practicing that profession, I have learned the value of having a familiar and dependable handbook for ready reference.

That was the intent of preparing this manual. It is recommended that you read it through once, to become familiar with the resource. The index, chapter titles, and sub-headings are intended to make it easy to quickly and accurately go directly to the subject at hand and find an answer to your questions.

Be aware, I am not suggesting you will find the answer to every question. If you do, it may not be the only answer. In addition, it may not even be the *right* answer. The *right* answer, of course, is the answer that accomplishes *your* purpose.

Many answers from my engineering handbooks were specific, based upon mathematics, physics, and chemistry. Answers to questions concerning family reunions do not always fit into a formula. There are just too many variables. We recognize that each family may have a different *right* answer to the same question. These forty years have taught us that successful family reunions are more art than science.

However, many things are common among the choices that cause family reunions to become long-term, successful traditions.

The answers and suggestions in most of these chapters are based upon the specific, first-hand experience of forty years of trial-and-error of our particular family. While this family was spawned in the Midwest (Southern Indiana), the five generations involved now are from thirteen states— from Connecticut to California, Alaska to Hawaii.

Chapter nine offers suggestions from friends and acquaintances, some of which we have not been able to test. They are believed to be very successful when they are thoughtfully applied.

In addition, *Secrets*…has been kept concise to provide a ready reference. Each chapter has enough white space for you to summarize ideas that are worth trying in your specific situation.

Your best reference will be this book after you have filled all margins and blank spaces with notes of ideas that occur to you as you study it. Notes should vary from "worth trying," "modify it like this," "not for us," to "great." In any case, your thoughtful additions will increase its value to you.

We are hopeful that this information can add to your success in family reunions, as well as to all your family relationships in general. If so, we will consider our efforts worthwhile.

Without wishing to be overly dramatic, we believe that the strength of our nation hinges upon the strength of our families. We can influence our culture, one family at a time. May your family and ours have positive influence!

For *our families* and for *our nation, good luck,* and *Godspeed*!

Your suggestions can help make this handbook even better. We invite you to send them to us.

Successful Family Reunions
P.O. Box 439, Ellington, CT 06029

Fax: 860-394-3030

E-mail:
http://www.successfulfamilyreunions.org/contact.html

Visit our website:
http://www.successfulfamilyreunions.org

Ten Reasons to Have Family Reunions

Secret Number One:
Family reunions offer the best opportunity to reinforce family values.

> Coming together is a beginning. Keeping together is progress. Working together is success.
>
> Henry Ford

"I can't wait to see Elizabeth this year—with the new baby!"

"Do you really want to go again this year?"

"Mom, do I have to go?"(said with the appropriate "teenager's whine").

Family reunions—love them or hate them, we feel drawn to them.

The family reunion, well planned, well conducted, and with full participation, can accomplish many good things. In this handbook we will share details of how one nuclear family has done this effectively. We have had our challenges. However, since 1946 we have planned and executed annual family gatherings from all across the nation for more than forty consecutive years.

A number of our friends have expressed their dismay. "Why would you possibly want to do that?" But even more of our friends have wistfully said, "I wish we could do that!"

In order to maintain our long run of success, several of our family members have been deeply involved in the long-term planning, giving serious consideration to every aspect of family reunions.

Before we talk about the *how*, let me offer to help you understand the *why*. Make no mistake; it requires serious effort and equally important, thoughtful, strategic planning. Our experience has taught us that even with the effort required, the *Results Are Worth It*!

WHY WOULD ANYONE COME TO A FAMILY REUNION?

There are lots of reasons; some easily come to mind:

1. The cousins have fun together.
2. Relationships are built and strengthened.

Some reasons can be kind of shallow: *(and we all think this way...sometimes)*

3. Let's show off the new car.
4. Did Cousin Ann get fat—like her mother?

If we think a little more in depth, the reasons just get better and better:

5. Everyone gets to see and understand the uniqueness of their own family history.

6. Children gain insight in to the different jobs and professions of different family members.

7. The development of a support system for young or struggling families is continued.

8. The marriages in the family can be strengthened.

9. Shared faith in the family can be easily encouraged.

10. Grandchildren are taught to respect the legacy their Grandparents left.

11. Younger generations come to understand the price that some of our family paid for our freedom.

12. Contributes to the youngsters' understanding of how difficult it was to keep the family together during the "Great Depression" years of 1929 and 1930.

Reunions have been around for thousands of years. There must be some reason that people keep having reunions even though reunions are not always successful.

Let's look in more detail at some of the results of well-planned family reunions. We believe the following ten ways a family reunion can impact, inspire, and pass on the important family attributes are enough to warrant significant effort.

IMPACT ON FAMILY FUTURE

As we grow older and/or more successful, we begin to wonder about our influence on future generations. Thinking of our family legacy is natural. No one event broadens or solidifies your family legacy more than the family reunion.

The reunion broadens it by allowing you to compare and measure it with families that in general come from similar backgrounds and are likely to have similar values.

As you compare and sharpen your values, they become more firmly entrenched. This intensifies the family desire to pass these assets, undiminished, to future generations.

We feel the usual viewpoint that legacy is made up entirely of material assets is much too narrow. In fact, we do not feel it is the most important asset you bequeath to your offspring.

Chuck Colson has made the point in his book *The Good Life* that the "worldview" developed and transmitted is of extreme importance to us, our family, and the world at large. See www.successfulfamilyreunions.org to get a copy of this book for a very helpful study.

Detailed handling of the family legacy is beyond the scope of this book. However, it is of sufficient importance that the author has a substantial report on this subject in draft for those who are interested.

IMPACT ON OUR YOUTH

All of us are aware that we live in a very negative environment. News bulletins, newspaper headlines, work situations, sports leaders, and celebrities—the list goes on.

Our youth are exposed to the same thing plus their own negative influences. They are even more influenced by bullying, trash talk, ultra-competitive situations, etc. Unless we make a special effort, this is interpreted as the norm and has marked effect upon their attitudes.

Even one week or long weekend each year can illustrate that there is a different and more pleasant way to live. Their desire to belong is strong, which allows us to strengthen that family bond.

Some ask, "You mean that one time a year will protect them from drugs, gangs, and all?" Of course, that alone in a very negative environment is no guarantee. The Reunion will, however, be a strong support to those families looking for as many positive influences as possible to support their family values.

Impact on Marriage

It is always of great interest to the extended family, and some concern as well, to see the lifemate a young person chooses.

Usually the young family member will, after becoming "serious" about a prospective mate, bring them to a reunion prior to an engagement. It is an opportunity that works to the advantage of both. It goes without saying that the visitor is treated with respect and sensitivity. However, it is probably more important for the visitor to observe how family members treat each other.

You can see that this can be a useful experience. Prior to reaching the stage described above, some value judgments are considered. The opportunity to see how other married couples cope is at least as useful as formal learning experiences.

IMPACT ON A SUPPORT SYSTEM

Many of our youth see no need for a family support group. Most have yet to experience how rapidly their peer group evaporates upon graduation and how difficult it is to maintain contact and interests with our once-close friends.

Even many young parents, who know the need for physical help with small children, become so busy they give little thought to the stability given by a caring family who remain interested in their welfare over an extended period.

However, by the time children have reached adulthood, most parents have experienced enough trauma in their family to have given up the childish "look, Mom, no hands, I can do it myself" attitude. Men especially have a difficult time admitting that. Our macho instincts are strong. We eventually learn that our bravado does not solve our problems.

At some time in our life we will meet situations where the help, interest, and understanding of a caring family will give us assistance and comfort that is available nowhere else.

The following story is from my own personal experience, while traveling on business. While none of us plan such episodes, the variables of family life are likely to cast us in the role of receiving such assistance. If we are fortunate, we will also have opportunity to give such assistance.

"Your wife has been rushed to the hospital for an emergency operation, not life threatening, but you are to return home at once." The comment greeted me late at night after a late flight and a long drive from Cleveland,

Ohio, to a business meeting in a small town in Northern Arkansas.

With no evening return flight, a private plane got me back to Cleveland about daybreak. From midnight to daybreak my thought centered on my wife. *How is my wife? How will I juggle her needs and our family needs?* Two children were in grammar school, one in high school, and my demanding job—all in a town we had moved to less than six months before.

After attending to the immediate needs, I called my older sister living 300 miles away. This brought an immediate response. "Bob, my children are old enough to care for themselves. I'll be right over to help."

It is difficult to describe the relief these words brought.

LEGACY OF CHARACTER ASSETS

Family culture is considered the accumulation of behaviors and belief that characterize a family.

These are made up of such traits as attitudes, values, customs, and expectations that define the lifestyle of such a group.

These attributes are assets that allow for common mission and an orderly way to manage or administer our lives. These attributes are the major factors in keeping culture intact and adding value over years and even generations.

Character assets are usually even more important than the material assets themselves. The best instruction we know of is that given by Mr. Williams in *Philanthropy, Heirs and Values*. For those interested in a copy, one can be obtained through **www.successfulfamilyreunions.org**.

Legacy of Faith Assets

While we come from a devout Christian family, we are by no means perfect. The Gathering gives all an opportunity to review the changes that have occurred in our lives and opens the subject of faith as a subject for legitimate discussion.

This would be of equal importance to members of any faith where the desire is to encourage the continuation of the family faith heritage. This could be done in many different ways, but it needs to be done thoughtfully with respect and concern for others who may have acquired different beliefs.

In the early years of our Gathering, we attended a local church service on Sunday morning. In the very early days we would march in to a local church thirty-five or forty strong and double the congregation of our "home" church near The Farm.

Soon we started holding our own family service with music, scripture, message, etc.—all from family members. Everyone feels it a major challenge to share and to some extent advise others in an environment where each of our foibles and weaknesses are so well known. This willingness for heartfelt sharing is universally appreciated.

Legacy of Material Assets

Material assets consist of personal property and real estate, businesses, and operating ventures as well as money and negotiable paper.

These are convenient to be evaluated by accountants and transmitted to future generations by attorneys through wills and trusts. Too often these are treated in strict mechanical fashion instead of giving careful thought, meeting equal needs as opposed to treating all exactly alike.

It is interesting to contemplate the data gathered by Roy Williams of The Williams Group, who has studied more than 3000 families with substantial material assets to bequeath.

Their studies showed that of those whose wealth was lost to the family in one generation, only 30% lost it because of poor accounting or legal advice.

The majority (70%) lost their material assets as a result of inadequate preparation in relational skills—not a common set of values or mission. Family members simply had not gained the skills and attitudes required to handle money or resolve differences as a unit.

Insight into

Jobs or Professions

Every child during their growing years chooses many heroes—and changes them often. In that way they think about many ways of finding a satisfying life's work.

Most boys go through stages of cowboy, airline pilot, race car driver, or construction worker early in life. Girls consider teaching, nursing, acting, or singing, and more recently, business or technical professions.

Later they consider their parents' lifework or the profession of a favorite teacher/mentor. Those are all good, but still have a very narrow focus. Worse yet, most information they get is biased and very superficial.

At a family reunion, children are exposed to many work/

lifestyles in much more depth than they get from their high school counselors. They see the pattern over several years and the effect of several different jobs on adult stress, children's reaction, and other family changes. Does the job require travel? How do other members of the family look at various jobs?

Does this job in Industrial Plant Management require or offer frequent family moves? Does the Attorney job Aunt Sally liked so well as a young single and newly married still fit as she becomes the mother of two kids?

Is teaching much more stressful than we realized? All of this occurs in an environment where the observations can be easily discussed. This discussion can easily be at the child level and between Parent and Child during the coming year.

Insight into

Various Lifestyles

As important as selection of a job or profession is, it is vastly more important for children, as they mature, to have insight into various lifestyles. While they get some insight from their peer group and their peers' parents, it is much more superficial than the exposure within the extended family.

Although their parents might know a little about the actual lifestyle, values, and goals of their friend's parents, it is certainly not enough to explain, with any accuracy, the visible changes within the family.

On the other hand, adult brothers and sisters who remain close will share deeply. When a child asks why

Uncle Fred quit his job or Aunt Beth has no children, it provides a good opportunity for a parent to have a discussion on values. Keeping in mind that confidential matters remain so, there is much helpful information that can be shared, appropriate to the age level.

To learn that a respected relative quit a job or was fired due to a conflict of values and is respected even more by the extended family can give a young adult courage to solidify his/her values early in life. Alternately, recognition of the penalty of a false step or poor moral choice can also be a significant learning experience for a child, if handled by the parent with integrity and sensitivity.

In any case the knowledge and insight from extended family interaction gives a much broader experience to growing children than just their nuclear family. Also, greater depth is allowed than the formal input by schools, etc. While formal input is valuable, it is enhanced greatly by close, family interaction.

Internalizing
of Family History

It is one thing to hear or read the family history. Both are useful. However, nothing is like actually witnessing it or, better yet, living it for a while.

We have illustrated how useful the family reunion is to inform children of how their family has lived, the jobs held by heads of families to put "bread on the table," and common recreation of past generations.

The possibilities are endless!

At one early reunion much time was spent in showing grandchildren how the grandparents lived. They knew them mostly as retired workers. Our experience is that great grand-children are too far removed for this to hold their attention.

One aunt, using the tools (strainer, crocks, etc.) demonstrated how milk was cared for on a farm with no refrigeration; another actually made noodles from a family recipe—from scratch. The dough was rolled, cut, and unrolled—shaped like linguini, only better tasting. A third showed the sewing skills and discussed the making of shirts, etc.

The men's skill demonstrations included a discussion on how coal was mined in shaft mines (deep wells). They had the actual tools used, including a pick with a handle of Osage orange, actually made by hand (and used) by my dad, the Patriarch of the Clan.

Others illustrated how corn was cut, shocked, and shucked. Another showed how white-oak shingles were rived with a family froe, also hay cutting, stacking, and hauling prior to the use of balers.

In all of this, someone who had worked with a "practitioner of the craft" actually did the work with younger generations having hands-on experience.

Family Insights
Are Much the Same

As a farm boy in the Midwest in the 1930s and early '40s, I grew up with the farms on either side owned by my mother's siblings, each with a family similar to ours. I watched and worked with my uncles and older cousins in hayfields, wood lots, and other farm activities. I saw a blacksmith at work and was close to men working the "top" jobs at coal mines where coal was cleaned and sorted by size. Best of all, everyone in the community knew us, and our obligation to represent the family set most of our values.

To my surprise, several years ago, I heard variations of this same story from a NYC cabbie moving to Florida because the community where he had grown up in Brooklyn had lost a sense of unity. No longer aunts and uncles in the same two blocks. The Men's Club where he "grew up" no longer contained men of like minds. I was astounded
that his feeling of the extended family matched mine so closely.

Keys to Secret One:

1) Goals need to be established, agreed upon, and understood by all responsible parties.

2) Use short, interesting stories to convey family values.

3) Intentionally work with the younger generations to develop interest in and respect for the extended family.

4) Purposefully develop an understanding of the family values.

How to Start a Family Reunion

Secret Number Two:
The first event must be well attended and universally enjoyed.

> Get a good idea and stay with it. Dog it, work at it until it's done, and done right.
>
> Walt Disney

"We would like to do that. How did you get started?"

This is the most common question we hear when people find out that our family has been holding reunions for more than forty years.

Some people who ask this question don't really want much of an answer. A simple "Well, it takes some planning" is enough to end their curiosity. Fortunately, others like you (since you are reading this book) really want to know more in order to make a positive difference in their family.

Ten General Guidelines

There are, of course, many ways to start. We will share our own specifics, since we know them best, and then identify a few other ways. However, here are some general principles:

1. It is good to select a specific event or milestone to build around—a wedding, an anniversary, a birthday, any local celebration, etc.

2. Be sure the event is of near-equal interest or importance to all the family.

3. Informally talk the prospect of a meeting with several key leaders of individual segments of the family.

4. Do not dwell upon the expectation that the Gathering will be an annual event. No one wants to feel obligated long term until it has been proven successful.

5. Announce approximately one year in advance. Announcement should only formalize what most already know.

6. Get maximum participation in the planning and preparation. This is a good way to build ownership.

7. Consider specific needs of various age groups. They are different. Be sure to have something for all. Make certain that everyone has an enjoyable time—so they will want to repeat it.

8. Include the proper amount of "free time" so everyone does not feel rushed or driven. Depending on interests and availability, a Saturday afternoon to shop, golf, fish, or just reminisce can be very refreshing.

9. Most of all, be sure to give some form of recognition or sense of accomplishment to each individual.

10. Keep the environment upbeat with no sniping, individual put downs, etc.

Of course, significant planning needs to be done prior to the decision and the announcement. A brief review of how our family progressed may be helpful.

EARLY FAMILY GATHERINGS

With seven children, spread over twenty-two years, early family gatherings consisted of the return of those "out of the nest" on vacations or holidays.

The Matriarch was the central contact point and made sure all were advised and encouraged to return anytime. Special emphasis was made when we could all be together. No effort was too great for those remaining on the Farm, when a Gathering was on the schedule.

Returning siblings had their favorite foods prepared and other forms of recognition. They, in turn, brought gifts for the family or individuals as appropriate.

This was a modest six-room country home, and all incomes were modest, but sharing and thoughtfulness was the key. The home was crowded, the activity was high, but with all sharing, the fun and laughter was infectious.

EARLY REUNIONS

Perhaps the first "real reunion" occurred after World War II. After a hiatus caused by the war—with two brothers and one brother-in-law in the army, one brother in the Navy, and an Airman as an ardent suitor of a sister—we felt the need to gather. Those from Michigan and California stayed at The Farm. With three siblings living within driving distance, accommodations were easily arranged.

After some intermittent, partial Gatherings, a significant reunion was planned in 1954. By that time one family was on the West coast, one on the East coast, and the remainder in various locations, mostly in two Midwestern states.

The Farm was the natural setting for the Gathering. Four trailers in the unused barn lot, two families in the Farm Home, and one couple, experienced campers, in a tent on the back lawn. Some food from the Farm kitchen, together with picnic-style meals, gave maximum time for fellowship and sharing. Stays were three to five days depending upon the practicality of job pressure and travel plans.

With careers to establish and families starting to expand, the distance caused full family reunions to be less frequent than we liked. In the late '50s the daughters recognized that the fiftieth wedding anniversary of our parents was set to occur in 1960, which merited a major celebration. All joined in the planning.

It was recognized that nothing would please the Honored Guests as much as a family reunion. To accomplish this a full week at the Farm was planned. How to do this without taxing (too much) the Matriarch, who always felt full responsibility for the output of her farm kitchen, caused much sibling discussion.

It was agreed that no cooking would be done in the Farm kitchen. The only exception made was to assist the catering on the Sunday of the celebration when relatives and neighbors were invited for the afternoon.

SPECIAL PLANNING
FOR INTERACTION

A cook shack and dining room were simply constructed with wood framing, a wainscot of masonite, screen wire above, and a plastic roof. A gas stove was installed with a stainless-steel sink and a work table, along with tables and chairs. All these were from a "going out of business" restaurant. This Cook Shack, flanked with five house trailers lined up in the shade of a row of sassafras trees, made our goal possible.

One single sibling and one couple with the newest family addition stayed in the Farm House with the Central Couple. All ate together with meals cooked by family members. A duty roster was posted for the week with two couples assigned to cook each day with two youth assigned to assist. Agreed-upon menus were prepared. This was made possible by the Central Couple's desire, the work ethic of all family members, and enormous effort of one sister, whose family lived thirty miles away and prepared the outdoor facilities.

While it would have been possible to hire cooks or have meals catered, the fellowship of having the family togetherness with no outsiders was worth the extra effort. This arrangement was mostly about old times and reliving past relationships. It was also helpful to include spouses in those relationships. At the end of the week, all agreed it was a huge success.

Following that, joint meetings at the Farm and in each other's homes were as frequent as possible with growing families and job requirements.

THE FIRST OF
THE ANNUAL REUNIONS

During this time, the Family Reunion was discussed with desire and intensity increasing as the years progressed. The impetus to bite the bullet and get started was generated by the Patriarch's eightieth birthday in 1967. Although the West Coast family was not able to attend, the other six, with all grandchildren, met for a long weekend at an Indiana state park that offered suitable facilities and a central location.

Plans were such that all enjoyed it immensely. Most of the third generation were the age that allowed parents to drive the entire family cross-country. The siblings (second generation) realized that this fellowship was too important to leave to chance; now was the time to inaugurate annual reunions.

With games, recognition, and family warmth, the planners made sure all had something to enjoy. Of course, many other events that draw families together could be of equal value as a beginning.

- Weddings: Often these are very important family gatherings with representatives of all wings of the family present. This would be a good opportunity to start the family reunion planning.

- Local Community celebrations: Church reunions, high school reunions, historical recognition events, etc., could also be effective starting points.

- Funerals: Yes, even funerals. These often account for the largest gathering of the extended family. In addition, these often are times when togetherness and family unity can be at its maximum.

Why Funerals Can Be Better than Weddings

Some years ago a Jesuit Priest told me he disliked weddings but liked funerals. I asked why he felt that way; he summed up his feeling by saying, "In most weddings the clergy is not wanted but needed. The Church is wanted for the beauty and convenience of the Sanctuary, not for the faith symbols or meaning. At a funeral the Clergy is needed for comfort and understanding. The family is talking freely in meaningful terms about the past and thinking about the future. They are open to faith, forgiveness, and family togetherness and that seems to be of major importance."

This could be an ideal time to make serious plans for a family reunion.

Strike while the Iron Is Hot

(But be sure the iron is well prepared)

Any of the above or similar gatherings can be effectively used to inaugurate a family reunion, if there has been proper preparation.

Each generation has a few pro-active members who are seen as "thought leaders." These should be involved in an advanced discussion. Not to manipulate or control, but to confirm that this is an opportune time. Also, to check if there are complications such as pregnancies, wedding plans, etc., since no one person can know all of the possible deterrents, most favorable time, etc.

If there is some consensus in this group, then it should be discussed in open forum in the full family gathering. A consensus of the full group, with enthusiastic support from the thought leaders will be effective. It will be especially effective if one of the thought leaders is able to cast an attractive vision of the "why" as described in chapter one.

Without this kind of preparation a first meeting will usually result in general agreement but not positive action. It can then be difficult to keep momentum until positive action can be agreed upon.

Announce Early and Often

Promptly after the length of time and date is decided upon a written notice should go out to all who are invited. This needs to be upbeat, contain a save the date message, but include a brief description of the why and those who participated in the decision.

A brief survey sheet should be included to encourage participation and know what will be attractive to the attendees.

1. Will you be there? Yes___ Likely___ Uncertain___

2. What are you most looking forward to?

3. Are there special activities you would like us to include?

4. Can you help with ideas, occasional contacts, planning food, etc?

Leave space for answers. Then, follow-up with meaningful things they can do to assist. Plan enough to keep them interested, but don't bug people too often.

Be sure your correspondence portrays a great event, with food, fun, and fellowship.

Keys to Secret Two:

1) Starting event should be a known attractor for a wide audience.

2) Family thought leaders should be involved in early planning.

3) Announce date, location, etc. in an upbeat manner, far in advance—one year ideally.

Where to Hold the Family Reunion

Secret Number Three:
The location must support the reunion objective.

> Absorb ideas from every source.
>
> Thomas Edison

"Uncle John's farm was an ideal location for our family reunion. But he and Aunt Sally are getting older and can't do it anymore. Looks as if we need to drop it."

Fear Not! The next right place can be found.

Families:

An Ever-Changing Stream

It is good to expect that conditions will change. As in a flowing stream, you can look upstream and see the future. You can look ahead and see the likelihood of necessary changes. Recognize that more than one location can support a successful event. Review your goals. Remember that the location must match the interests and goals of the group.

With our family, the primary goal was continual bonding and togetherness. Therefore, we felt a necessity for private meeting space, separate eating facilities, and room for group games. These were considered equal in importance to adequate sleeping facilities.

Again we will look at some of our history and then consider other suggestions.

Early Reunion Locations

As previously described, during the early days on the Farm, family members did 100% of the cooking and cleanup. With proper scheduling and pairing of family work parties, it added to the fellowship.

When that became too difficult, we moved to a State Park, which worked well for a few years. However, as the dining room management staff became very hard to work with, facilities aged, and new family members were added, it became less attractive.

Our next move was to a church camp, which had less desirable sleeping facilities; but the privacy, spacious grounds, and right-sized meeting rooms for our family were a good fit. That lasted for a few years.

Returning to the state park became attractive again when we found a stand-alone meeting room facility that could be available. It was located apart from the main lodge that had been renovated, allowing the privacy we enjoy.

Years at the Church Camp

One year, we did go back to the Farm House and cook shack, mostly for sentimental reasons; we learned that the effort of preparing the now-vacant home and grounds for forty to fifty people was too much work for a once a year event.

In searching a wide area central enough to meet our needs, a suitable church camp was located. The schedule was perfect. The camp summer schedule was complete the week prior to Labor Day. The Board of Directors met at noon on Labor Day, so the camp needed to remain open. However, it was empty and without income.

Since our schedule had shifted to Labor Day, to accommodate the older youth who worked summer jobs and to allow an additional day for travel, we meshed together well. The family had a private facility to plan the activities we wanted without interference.

A cook staff was responsive to our desires at a reasonable price. The camp had income from forty to fifty guests arriving on Friday afternoon or evening and leaving on Monday morning. Since all had miles to travel there was no interference with the noon luncheon followed by a Board Meeting. It was a good fit!

Improved State
Park Accommodations

A few years at the church camp, accompanied by growing families, generated a need for different facilities. This prompted a move back to the state park.

Fortunately, the park lodge had been totally renovated but had not yet become popular as a family reunion venue. We were able to rent a stand-alone hut suitable for several private meals, headquarters for games, church services, and free-time visiting. Rental cabins could serve a similar purpose.

This location is now ideal for the sixty to sixty-five people regularly attending. It has the privacy we desire and facilities for the activities to meet the needs of the diverse ages and interests of second, third, and fourth generations. It also has great memories for the second and third generations who first assembled there forty years ago.

The popularity of this location for family reunions and the changing methods of reservations may require our family to consider other options in the future.

This is intended to show you what has worked for one family. Clearly, there is a need to have criteria for selection, be aware of changing needs, and adapt as needed to what is available.

While we view state parks very favorably, recommend them highly, and have included extensive state park helps in the Reunion Planning Toolkit (see Resource Pages), state parks are by no means the only successful locations for family reunions.

COMMERCIAL MOTELS/HOTELS/RESORTS

You have heard our family's experience, but we know that family goals and interests vary greatly.

Many successful reunions are held at motels, hotels, and resorts, all of which provide many advantages.

There is literally an unlimited number of these facilities in the US, and they can be found everywhere. They also offer a wide range of prices, services, and support staff.

While motels tend more to rural locations and hotels to urban, they overlap enough to defy any clear categorization.

Resorts tend to be more specialized and offer more activities to appeal to a broader group. They have the potential to also offer more interference with your schedule and family activities. *Care should be taken to be sure their attractions contribute to and do not detract from your family objectives.*

Some families are large and meet on a two, three, or five-year schedule. When family groups exceed a few hundred (some are 1000 plus), they often organize quite formally with a national organization made up of regional officers, etc. Often the regional groups meet annually quite informally, while the entire national group meets for large formal occasions on less frequent intervals. These are most often convened in large, urban hotels where commercial transportation is available. The assistance in planning offered by such hotels should be used. They have excellent services to assist.

Many locations allow for educational and entertainment experiences. The variety of historical events are limited only by your families' interests and desires. If in Philadelphia, incorporate Constitution Hall and the Liberty Bell; if in Boston, visit the Freedom Trail; if in Atlanta, venture to the Cyclorama and the Great Train Ride display.

Others cities provide historic experiences, including

elements of Southern Heritage, Civil War history, the History of the West, the legends of the Black Hills, and enough other things to suit any interest.

Major hotels have learned the power of the family reunion, recognize its importance as an income producer, and are willing to make attractive offers of discount pricing, facility accommodations, and planning assistance in order to attract your group.

Don't hesitate to discuss with them, early on, dates that can be attractive to both you and your preferred housing provider. Be sure to have your records of the last three to five years available on how many rooms you block out versus how many you actually use. They may check the hotel to confirm this. They are favorably influenced by dependable and desirable family reunions.

Your good record and desirability as a dependable customer gives you great strength in negotiating better rates and other services.

BED & BREAKFAST FACILITIES

Do not overlook the possibility of using a B&B as an ideal location for your family reunion. The number and variations of these make it impossible to offer much in the way of meaningful specifics. Usually small-to-medium-sized reunions could book the entire facility and have a private club atmosphere.

These vary from simple to quite upscale, from inexpensive to quite expensive. Usually, as is often the case, you get what you pay for. Any library will have directories for B&Bs, usually regional, and will have descriptions, room numbers, and phone numbers. Most are single-proprietor owned and are very helpful to potential reunion planners.

OTHER STATE PARKS

Many states have parks with similar facilities where a very economical family reunion can be planned. Privacy can be enjoyed, and enough activities are available to suit your particular family situation.

After a few years experience with our Wolfe Family Reunion, our son-in-law began a reunion with his own family, and they found a different setup that works great for their group.

Coming from Connecticut, Georgia, and Pennsylvania, a park in West Virginia fits their needs well. Instead of a lodge, they choose three individual cabins in close proximity of each other. One is large enough for the group to gather for meals, meetings, and indoor games. This cabin is always occupied by the Chair Family who serves as hosts. This arrangement has been very successful for the last fourteen years.

PRIVATE, COMMERCIAL, THEME PARKS

One year our Chair Family chose a regional theme park built around an Amish lifestyle. It was necessary to have a "headquarters" tent erected as a place to gather so as to conduct the business and conversation desired. A pleasant change of pace surprised us, and we had a very successful reunion. Other theme parks could work equally well.

This was very successful for one year, exposed us all to a different culture, and required a different kind of planning. However, not enough variety was available to sustain enthusiasm for several years, therefore it did not lend itself to the same "togetherness" we had experienced elsewhere.

PRIVATE YOUTH
OR SPORTS CAMPS

Every area has a number of youth and/or sports camps. Many of these have an off week usually either early or late in the season. This can be caused by difficulty in obtaining staff, guest booking, or the desire of management.

They usually have adequate kitchen and cook staff, good meeting rooms, facilities for games, great sports facilities, etc. More planning is required, and the likelihood of that week or long weekend closing up is greater than commercial rentals. But with planning around these limitations, and recognizing common interests, these can be very successful.

PRIVATE HOMES

Today, many private homes are of sufficient size to accommodate the entire extended family, though usually not without inconvenience to the owner. This is especially true if the space or an area nearby allows the boys or families experienced in camping to expand the sleeping facilities.

This or any of the above, especially state or commercial parks, can be combined with RVs or trailers, if they are available. If these are not owned by family members, they are for rent in most areas.

LOCAL PARKS, COMMUNITY HOUSES, AND PICNIC AREAS

It is safe to say that all communities have local parks available for picnics and other activities, usually with sports facilities. Almost always, table reservations are possible, sometimes with covered pavilions. Since planning ahead is essential and weather is unpredictable, weather protection should be considered.

These parks offer an excellent opportunity for an afternoon or all-day gathering of family members if members live nearby. For those living farther away, it usually requires arranging for sleeping facilities. This can be with family members, motels, or camping facilities nearby.

Often distant-family members can stay with relatives and have a successful one or two-day experience.

While a one-day event can renew acquaintances and be a fun day for children, in our experience it lacks the opportunity to build long-term interests or transmit family values and culture as longer, well-planned programs provide.

Our first and second-generation family members had many years of two or three Gatherings per year. Many of us, with families of our own, returned to the reunion often more out of obligation to parents than personal desire.

Those who wanted to spend their time visiting and renewing acquaintances enjoyed it. Kids enjoyed swings, slides, and sports, depending on age. Others found it a burden to listen to a dry history lecture on family and town from Judge Martin L. Pigg, a distant family relative.

Summary

The family I grew up in was a farm-and-coal miner family of modest means. There were no extravagant expectations, the family work ethic was strong, and the most important objective was to make the reunion available to all without financial burden.

Therefore, most of our actual experiences have been at inexpensive locations with simple menus. There is usually some food preparation by family members. We universally prefer "our own" to that available in any restaurant we know.

The Saturday salad luncheon has become famous. The troops would likely mutiny if that were omitted. Arranged on the tables is the widest array of salads imaginable, topped off with the three aunts' fruit cobblers—each specializing in a different fruit!

To recap our adventures, here is a list of actual experience of my family:

- Family Farm: A place loved by all, no interference from outside influences, plenty of room to roam, great memories. It did require detailed planning, not a wide variety of activities, and not centrally located.

- State Park (Indiana): Both before and after it became a major lodge and conference center, it became an excellent location for our purpose. It requires great care in registering and continual adaptation to changing rules.

- Church Camp: This worked well for a while. Provided good grounds, suitable meeting rooms, good kitchen, and dining facilities. Also was very economical. Lacked much in room cleanliness and activity variety.

- Regional, Private Theme Park: Nice variation from the pattern; an interesting culture. Did not have suitable meeting rooms readily available. Not enough activities for long-term interests and did not offer the privacy our family enjoys.

Other venues of interest:

- Private youth and sports camps

- Private homes

- Local Parks and Community Houses

This is not an exhaustive list, but it does offer enough different locations to illustrate the need for careful selection and flexibility. Obviously no one-type location would fit all.

Keys to Secret Three:

1) Evaluate facilities against family goals.

2) Consider needs of all generations.

3) Get input from the maximum number of those involved.

4) Change locations *only* after thoughtful consideration.

Ways of Organizing and Scheduling

Secret Number Four:
A successful and proven model can be adapted to your needs.

> Before everything else, getting ready is the secret of success.
>
> Henry Ford

"Why does everything need to be planned so carefully? I'd just like to visit a while." This comment came from an older member of the planning group.

We do not mean to suggest that the entire reunion be a froth of activity. It is important that planning be intentional and considerate of all ages and interests. The key to continuing the ongoing reunion is held by our teenagers.

Boredom for our youth is the unforgivable error.

This generation is physically and mentally active. They are used to texting and instant messaging with their friends, information found at the click of a mouse, and waiting twenty minutes at the most for a pizza.

Yet there are times when the family gathers or when a meal finishes that are not suitable for planned activity. Here is time for individuals or paired activity. More ideas are presented later on specific activities, but remember: careful planning is essential.

Since you have read thus far, you know that successful reunions do not happen by accident. Any enduring legacy requires thorough planning and sustained effort.

USE A SUCCESSFUL MODEL

While there is more than one way to organize successfully, some commonalities among those procedures work well. It is helpful to plan your reunion around a successful model.

I will share our model with you from our more than forty years' experience. In less detail, I will share other models we have learned from those who have had experience with them.

Like most successful enterprises, the most effective organization is quite simple, but with complex overtones that may not be readily apparent.

First, there needs to be a leader. This needs to be a respected member of the family with enough energy and enthusiasm to project a successful conclusion to the effort. This should be someone who has maintained contact with the family over an extended period. Not someone "on the family periphery" who wants to demonstrate his or her ability to manage a one-man (person or family) show.

Secondly, a committee needs to be formed, either formally or informally, with the purpose of getting broad-based input, so that the needs of the entire family are understood, considered, and evaluated.

This does not mean "we do whatever we are asked." It does mean giving consideration to all suggestions, getting appropriate input from others, and deciding. It also means having a variety of activities so that the program flows well, is not too much of a burden, and *all* enjoy some significant part of it.

GIVE CARE TO HOUSEKEEPING NEEDS

The early decisions include the usual housekeeping ones.

The old saw that Rudyard Kipling made famous with this poem has been of great help to me:

> I have six honest serving men;
>   They taught me all I knew.
> Their names are What and Why and When,
>   and Where and How and Who.

It will pay you big dividends to memorize this little ditty.

What: Family Reunion is a given, since it is our subject.

Why: Discussed in detail in chapter one.

Where: Depends upon location of expected attendees—a central location to encourage maximum turnout, without undue effort. Will people drive or fly? Is it a place with variety of facilities to accommodate all ages and interests? How is food to be handled? More details in chapter three.

When: Choose a time that will encourage maximum attendance. This is nearly as important as making sure all attendees enjoy the event and good vibes are generated. Often a special kickoff event can be selected that will assure this result. Such an occasion might be an important birthday, anniversary, or similar occasion.

Be sure it is chosen around an occasion that will attract many of the target audience. In our case the eightieth birthday of the family patriarch was a known attractor.

Such an event has one other important attribute—it lends itself to early planning—which is very important. Do not try to hastily put something together, advertise it widely, and create expectations that cannot be met. In today's world, many plan a year ahead. It is easy to cause great disappointment for all if the people who "should" be present, and genuinely want to come, are previously committed.

Such an event (or a fiftieth wedding anniversary, etc.) does not arrive unexpectedly. A bit of forethought is very important. It is not necessary that it be on the actual date as long as all understand the reasons for the variation and are not overly sensitive.

In our case the birthday in September made for an acceptable drive. Six families with school-age children did not consider driving 200 to 500 miles an inconvenience.

In the above situation, several following years' reunions had been observed in August. But as the third generation began working summer jobs, attending extended summer camps, etc., it was moved to Labor Day. That has now become so fixed that everyone reserves that date; the facility is booked two years in advance. Any significant change would be very difficult.

How long the event will last is usually a matter that needs particular consideration. Enough time needs to be given to renew the strong bonds and to spend at least some one-on-one time with most family members. It must still fit the budget and time schedule of a wide majority. Remember that it is good to leave them wanting more.

Who: The proper invitees are also important. Some are quite obvious—the descendants and families of a certain couple. Or they may divide geographically considering those that have interest in this event.

Like many things, this will likely vary with each family and be impacted by the program and pattern of the reunion.

How: Our best advice on how to get started was the subject of chapter two. The remainder of this book addresses how to best plan, schedule, and execute a successful family reunion and how to perpetuate it as an ongoing institution.

SHARING THE PLANNING OPPORTUNITY/RESPONSIBILITY

In our particular situation, my parents, the central couple—first generation—were never an active part of the planning. Their children (my siblings) made up the planning committee, with the Chair rotating from the very early years.

As the third generation became mature enough to be involved, we earnestly solicited their views. Since we had, by this time, determined that we would like to have the reunion continue indefinitely, we tried to look ahead.

Fortunately, none of the second generation suffered unduly from the expectations of immortality (we were all willing to take our turn as well as help others). We knew that we must plan the transition of organizing and planning responsibility.

As an unexpected bonus, it turned out to be a good "excuse" for the responsible Chair Family to gather on three or four planning occasions. This also increased the family contacts by phone, fax, and e-mail. This gives reason and meaning for more frequent family meetings at this time.

The concept of Chair Family allowed for a natural progression of turning over the reins. At the start, the second generation presided as Chair. Later their roles shifted to consultants and troubleshooters. And now, as four of the seven siblings (second generation) have passed away, the concept continues to prove its worth. This succession has occurred without a hitch.

The roles of consultants and troubleshooters should not be overlooked. As the family grows larger and older or as locations change, schedules and programs need to be changed to compensate. Significant changes need to be thought through and tested. The original organizers are ideal for reviewing this.

Seven siblings growing up together learn to know each other well. They can speak *very* candidly to each other without any particular sensitivity. Each family understands the need to maintain past activities enough for the group to feel comfortable and yet change enough to avoid growing stale and to meet changing needs.

One of the siblings maintained throughout her life that if anyone would ask her a question about any significant life subject, and she could tell you how each of her siblings would react. No one ever doubted her on this. Such insight is nearly impossible as the family changes through marriage, births, different life experiences, etc.

Chair Families have great authority to change the pattern, but all are interested in and sensitive to feedback. Feedback most often comes in the form of "My concerns are...," "Have you considered...," or possibly in the form of "Bob, we need to drop that activity!" (See example in chapter five).

We understand that some other groups seem pleased with one family or small group doing the planning and execution year after year. If that works successfully for them, we won't disagree. We are just concerned that concentration of the preparation leads to bland repetition and boredom.

Repetition can result in burnout of the organizers. It also fails to engender the deep commitment throughout the family that we are seeking.

SCHEDULING THE DETAILS

Schedules have room for variation. There seems to be unlimited variations possible in the month, time of month, number of days, when to start and stop, how much time to have planned, and how much to leave free.

Yet, we believe once the schedule is reasonably well established, it is difficult to successfully negotiate a significant change. If you know what you are trying to accomplish, in the practicality of the situation—such as travel limitations, facilities, group mentality, etc,—some order will evolve.

Items Causing Upset

For us, though a two-day weekend in August seemed short, it worked until that schedule conflicted with the need of the third generation. When they graduated from high school and were working summer jobs, complications arose. It became evident their work interfered with attendance. Since most were able to leave their summer jobs prior to Labor Day, we were able to shift to Labor Day Weekend.

Fortunately, the bonds had been well enough established that all were able to change and the facility had not become too heavily booked.

The next major upset occurred when many colleges started the semester *prior* to Labor Day. This had been unheard of in the second generation's time, so much debate was held. Some just missed these first few days of school, which can be difficult when starting a new school. Some drove in and back with shortened time; some were flown in from colleges farther away. Most colleges have abandoned this plan, at least those with which we are associated.

Since then, high schools have started scheduling sports activities over Labor Day. We still persevere, always allowing for late arrivals, etc., but making an effort to let absent members know they are missed (sending notes, etc.).

Our Working Schedule

Our best schedule: Friday evening check in kicks off the weekend. Saturday and Sunday activities and some free time keep everyone busy and connecting. Monday morning breakfast ends the reunion.

The schedule is revealed in detail in the Planning Toolkit shown on the Resource Pages.

This gives two *full* days with Saturday afternoon free time, Sunday afternoon game time, and two long evenings. This fits well for our annual gathering but may seem short for those on two, three, or five-year schedules.

Free time has come to mean shopping at a local discount mall, golf, napping, renewing acquaintances, etc. In addition, it provides a brief respite for the Chair Family.

Games have come to mean those including all who want to be involved. Largely team building games from egg toss, three legged races, caterpillar walking, etc., are used. Old family games are sometimes used, like jacks and marbles. These games are little known by third generation, but trying them lets them see a part of the world of their parents. We always try to have some interesting, new excitement builders. More information is in the Planning Toolkit.

Our all-time favorite and most competitive game is the egg-toss contest. The two-person teams vary greatly. Teams are often made up of siblings, couples of all ages, or young pairs of cousins who quickly become fast friends. These young, same-gender pairs quickly give way, when one brings a new friend or spouse.

Make no mistake, planning and executing an interesting weekend for fifty to seventy people including theme, food, games, church service, appropriate interaction, and more is a real task. It is a burden cheerfully assumed by all families, but appreciated even more because of its infrequency. While all are glad to assist when a need is seen or when called upon, it is always clear who bears the responsibility. *Everyone* appreciates that!

Keys to Secret Four:

1) Consider family goals, resources, and interests; then compare needs with known models.

2) Get broad based input from family thought leaders.

3) Error on the side of simplicity and reasonable costs to be as inclusive as possible.

4) Do a complete review ("post mortem") promptly after the event and objectively evaluate.

Successful Programs and Activities

Secret Number Five:
Programs and Activities with 80% familiar/20% new provide both comfort and excitement.

> Your own resolution to succeed is
> more important than any other thing.
>
> Abraham Lincoln

"Do you think Uncle Bob will remember to bring the stilts?"

"Will the puzzles be there this year?"

In response to a riddle challenge, given at breakfast on the closing day, three college-age students made their parents drive back to the lodge (after they were already two miles on their way home) to confirm that they had come up with the right answer. (Of course that was before the age of cell phones.)

These real life questions and actions from our young adults remind us how to keep our youth engaged with the reunion.

The functions of programs and activities are woven together in such a way that overlapping and interweaving is inevitable.

Programs are meant to refer to the overall plan. Activities are meant to be the details of a specific game or event. Hopefully, in the end it will be clear what has worked for us and, even more importantly, why it is considered successful.

PROGRAMS—PART ONE:

In the first few years, programs developed with little thought other than to meet the needs of planners.

Family members seemed satisfied just to reminisce and renew acquaintances. While the stories were new to kids and spouses, they seemed to enjoy the unusual escapades, with all roundly chiding the one who was the "goat" of the story. Stories—such as when one brushed his teeth with Griffin Alwhite (shoe polish); or when one brother teased another until a shoe flew through the air, breaking a prized, uniquely-shaped window pane—were often a unifier of all ages.

However, even these stories wear thin to those not involved. Thus Saturday afternoon free time was started, with all expected to be present for both lunch and dinner at the appointed hours. Of course, those "on duty" had shorter breaks.

Early on, we found that there was never enough time to permit one-on-one time with all in attendance. To counter this we hit upon informal talks after dinner (breakfast and lunch also) with each family at an assigned spot. The senior family member performed as Master of Ceremonies for that family. The MC is charged with keeping the program moving and showing sensitivity as needed.

We wanted to have everyone's input. This was referred to as the persons "ticket" for their meal. At first this was just a report on each one's highlights of the past year and any unusual plans for the year to come. Later, a theme of the year was added. More on this subject can be found under *activities.*

This was very rewarding as everyone heard the basics of each other's activities. This allowed for congratulations and follow-up on specific items of interest. Gradually, as people felt more comfortable, most everyone participated. Often, people are threatened in jest that all are participating this year. However, no pressure is applied at the time of the ticket presentation.

Family History

There seems to be a common interest in the activities of the different generations. The second generation wants the third generation to understand how life has changed. This can be made interesting if thoughtful consideration is given to practical and realistic changes.

The age-old "we had to walk five miles to school, uphill each way, through deep snow" soon gets the contempt it deserves. However, actual facts of the activities of a typical work day, the sacrifices required by the family members during war, natural disasters, or traumatic experiences involving family members are usually appreciated by younger members.

Children invariably enjoy learning of the mistakes made by parents. These can be kept in a light vein and become a very good teaching tool enjoyed by all.

For our own nuclear family, we review some of the moves we made as a family—some eight moves to five states. These had varying effects upon each child. Showing sensitivity, even at a delayed date, can help. Also, some of our early nuclear family vacations on bicycles, canoes, backpacking, etc., became good memories to review.

For the extended family, more universal influences are required. Following are good examples that carry a lesson.

1) The commitment of a Grandfather who worked in the deep well mines (story told in an earlier chapter).

2) An Uncle who was a flyboy in WWII with some time on Tinian Island in the South Pacific. The hazards of life when the first two atomic bombs were assembled. Consider the stress of knowing that an error would evaporate the entire island.

3) Another Uncle who spent most of WWII on the western front in Europe.

After a particularly heavy fire-fight (fire-fight accurately describes the event) with the German enemy, during the Battle of the Bulge, he was the *only* one of a squad of eight to answer roll call.

Each of the above family stories need to be developed enough so that those listening grasp the significance of the situation. This depends largely upon the age and understanding of the listeners.

It can also be helpful to all to review the "work history" of various family members. It gives perspective to the life of a successful individual and the sometimes-difficult decisions made in early life to build a successful profession, business, or life. These usually come as a revelation to developing children.

Passing on Family Values

Reviewing how family values were developed is helpful to encourage the younger members to accept them as their own or modify them to fit within their present lifestyles.

Keeping them broad makes them applicable to more situations. Occasionally a truly heroic decision was made by an earlier family member that affected the generations that follow. These vary from the need to be self reliant and resourceful to matters of faith. We must not let such opportunities be overlooked. Examples of this are in chapter six.

General Interest

Programs that are informative, educational, and broadening can add zest to a schedule if carefully chosen. It must be remembered that programs should be those requested by several members or known to be of general interest.

They should not be included just because an enthusiastic instructor wants to teach! This usually needs a careful survey—person to person to establish true interest.

These can vary from beauty aids, health programs, scrapbooking, and art classes to entrepreneurial skills and much more. These work best when they are optional and more than one is scheduled simultaneously. These should be done only occasionally and made truly optional.

Having something special for the nine to thirteen-year age group can be challenging. With our farm background and outdoor bent, things with nature seem worthwhile with our family. These activities keep the youth happy and can be done in any location if a few adults are willing to give attention to the youth of the extended family.

As is often the case with this age group, just being together, keeping on the move, and seeing new things is enough to escape boredom. They love it!

One such excursion is a Nature Hike, better billed as an Animal Adventure. Any observant outdoorsman, Scoutmaster, hunter, or fisherman can find evidence of ten animals in a field or wooded section. Adding trees and plants can add value to the activity. Our youth are often amazed!

A Bird Spotting trip is another reliable adventure for all ages, adaptable to most all outdoor settings. Your group may have an accomplished Bird Watcher. If not, most State Parks have someone to lead such a group.

In both the above cases, let the youth contribute as much as possible. Be sure each contribution is recognized appropriately.

Actually we feel the lessons to be learned far exceed the obvious subject matter. It is a good time to bring into focus the natural order to our world that is not always apparent in our high-tech society. Seasons, weather, nature's cycles, and natural happenings are little influenced by the click of a mouse. Sometimes this is referred to as the Nature Deficiency Syndrome.

ACTIVITIES—PART TWO:

One of the ways to incorporate family history into the reunion is to make a long-range plan of interesting subjects. Ask appropriate family members to prepare a suitable presentation on these subjects.

These stories, if kept light and in good taste, can remind all of us how life and culture has changed. Also, they tend to remind us all that many changes are culturally based. Many of these are cyclical and not worthy of undue energy.

Our first annual reunion was built around the eightieth birthday of the first generation Patriarch. All but one of the second generation and most of the third generation were present. This was well recorded on 35mm color slides (the best of the time). These have been shown several times, a few years apart.

Each family can vary this to suit their interests; but be alert to the interest of the group—particularly the spouses and younger generations. One of the ways to do this is to have pictures of entire generations that have gone through various cycles of "fashion trends" or "hairstyles."

ACTIVITY CATEGORIES

In addition to family history and culture, activities fall into several different categories. They need to be thought of as such, for each fill a different need.

Group Games—Active intergenerational
Group Games—Sedentary intergenerational
IndividualActivities—Preferably intergenerational
Drama Activities—Various
Rainy Day—To be kept "on deck"

GROUP GAMES—ACTIVE

This is the heart of Sunday afternoon games. Designed mostly for youth of all ages, including children down to five-years-old, most of the older adults watch and form a loud cheering section.

Egg Toss: An old, well-known faithful—our favorite. Very competitive. Rules: Teams line up, partners facing each other ten feet apart. One RAW egg is given to each team. Throw to partner in unison. Step back one full step. Throw again. Tension builds when partners get sixty feet apart with unbroken eggs. An umpire is recommended to keep lines straight.

Objective: Be last pair with unbroken egg. (Watch for prissiest girl to catch egg above her head and add golden egg to her golden hair.)

Three-Legged Race: Use cloth sacks to pair right leg of one partner with left leg of other. Run to line and back.

Rules: Can only move forward when legs are in sack.

Objective: Usually arranged in two or more relay teams. First team to complete wins.

Relay Pass Teams: Can use beans on a knife, egg on spoon, cup of water with tablespoon measure, partly-filled balloon passed with chin, etc. Be creative!

Rules: Abide by the rules given by the game instructor for rules sometimes vary. Entire team must participate.

Objective: Complete tasks as assigned.

Bubble-Blowing Contest: Give each individual one or two pieces of bubble gum. Have three judges to avoid a tie.

Rules: All use the same brand of bubble gum. Give practice time, but all start at assigned time.

Objective: Blow largest bubble. Great to fill time while group gathers.

Human Sling Shot: Three persons per team. Bands of medical rubber tubing (two strands each, 48" long) are needed. Make a six-inch loop on one end of each. Tie other end to a soft, flat leather strap approximately 4"x8". Use like a sling shot: one person holding a loop (two loop holders), one holding the leather "pouch." Ammo is round balloons filled to about four inches in diameter with water (forty to sixty balloons required). Position a youth as a target approximately ten yards away. Target should ideally be standing on a stump or board for elevation and precision.

Rules: Target can't leave stump or board. Objective: Wet the target. Vigorous youth love it—great for last game as most are willing to be spectators if earlier games were properly active.

Be Creative! These are games our family enjoys. Many other similar games requiring teamwork are fun, and your family probably knows and enjoys them. Use them.

GROUP GAMES—SEDENTARY

We recommend these only in case of inclement weather. They may also fit if there is an uncommon interest in a special game (such as checkers, chess, monopoly) and an expert available for teaching.

Cribbage is an excellent "one-on-one" card game that

lends itself to competitive play among equals or a mentor/mentored relationship. Great for intergeneration interaction. Although a cribbage board adds to the pleasure, score can be kept with pencil and paper.

Rum, Euchre, Pinochle, Poker, and Bridge are played with regular decks. These games, in varying degrees, are time consuming and tend to reduce personal family interaction instead of contributing to it. Poker and Bridge tend to be the largest offenders for being obsessive and pleasurable only when played by near equals.

Innumerable board games are available with information and instruction. These, however, tend to restrict interaction rather than promote it.

Dominos is the best of the board games for being fun for different skill levels. Usually the players play more casually and allow room for interaction.

Our own family has not found card games or board games useful in the long weekend reunions. We prefer to concentrate on different activity as described throughout this book.

No doubt there are families with different time allotments and different interests that have a different experience. We only wish to emphasize the need to be constantly aware of the group dynamics of the activity.

INDIVIDUAL ACTIVITIES

This refers to activities that are done individually but actually lend themselves best to one-on-one competition or to mentor/mentored relationships.

These are often overlooked but fill a very important need for our youth, who sometimes find it difficult to keep engaged. Youth need something to fill each minute and are impatient when waiting for the group to gather or when they finish meals more rapidly than their elders.

These started with our family, based upon "toys" we learned on the Farm. These were made by our handyman father from scraps readily available. Your family may know different toys that would fill this void equally well.

These consisted of two pairs of stilts, two pairs of hoop and handles, heart and clevis and string puzzles. We basically thought these were invented by our Dad only to later find they were rather universally used when families made their own fun.

Now, of course, all are available for a price. We encourage the making of these within the family and furnish instruction for doing so. We widely promote the idea that if a child above ten years of age is not proficient in making and using stilts, hoops, and handles, and the two family puzzles their Grandparents have been negligent!

Since then we have added bolo or ladder golf and simple Tavern Puzzles.

Puzzles are always in a special recognizable basket near the dining table. More active games are always visible near the activity. We find that these may remain untouched until someone starts...then a group gathers, all wanting to try. Anyone with the simple skills required, who starts using these toys, soon has a group gathered around giving the opportunity to show and tell. Competition quickly builds.

DRAMA

This is as varied as the families involved and has taken many turns. In our family, it's never really repeated exactly although it continues to build and grow on appropriate occasions.

Drama began first as demonstrations of family activities, old-fashioned kitchen skills, use of outdated farm tools, hymn singing, musical instrument jamming, barbershop, and special singing of past family favorites.

More recently these have included talent shows, dance performances (one young gal is skilled in Irish dancing), musical productions, etc., to the enjoyment of both performers and spectators.

A two-hour, three-act play was performed by this extended family in 1932. It is much like the classic old melodramas but with more meat to it. We have discussed this several times and feel sure we could cast it well within the family (with parts being read).

This project is always available for some ambitious Chair Family.

Rainy Day

While we have been blessed with good weather, most of the time we are aware that a cold, rainy three days could dampen family enthusiasm.

Our preparation has included having coloring books and crayons available for children, extending talent shows, some family history discussion, and indoor scavenger hunts.

We now wish to encourage the use of teams, age mixed as appropriate, to hurriedly interview and present a "This is your Life" production for an older member.

Two or three teams could be commissioned and awards given for the best presentation.

The importance of mentioning this is to make certain

the possibility of a rainy day is recognized. Any of the sedentary activities could be used if minimal consideration is given in advance.

None of us want the reunion to end on a note of disappointment. Planning will avoid this even on a rainy day.

GENERAL GUIDELINES

1. Know your family. Resurrect old family games, activities, etc.

2. Apply the 80/20 rule. 80% of familiar activities for comfort, 20% of new for interest.

3. Have someone available as an expert on the toys, games, and activities. Doesn't need to be the "World Expert"—just proficient enough to explain and encourage others.

4. Keep the atmosphere upbeat and encourage friendly competition where possible.

5. Give awards wherever possible. Have something simple for all. Perhaps wrapped hard candies for all and a little something better (chocolate bar, etc.) for the winner or winning team. Use an award—plaque, large button to wear, hat or cap with inscription, or similar showy award. Give recognition wherever possible.

ANNUAL THEMES

Our sharing has been enhanced by selecting a theme as a part of activities for each gathering. We ask each member to give some reflection on the subject chosen.

A very early, perhaps the first theme, actually a demonstration, was performed exclusively by the second-generation members of "Life on the Farm." Since all those members had spent their life, through the teen years, on the same farm, it gave a story with great continuity.

Since all the third generation had visited and enjoyed the farm since infancy, it had an abiding interest for them also. These were live demonstrations with third generation participation where possible. It made some impression on young minds.

For more ideas on this idea, see details in the Reunion Planning Toolkit, Resource Pages.

LIFESTYLES OF YESTERDAY

This was a fun series of demonstrations for the second generation and held a high level of interest among the third generation. It was an opportunity to incorporate family history with actual demonstrations, showing products where applicable.

In our case, men showed how farm and coal mining work was done. The women demonstrated their mothers' work at home. It was an opportunity to recognize the value of the "homemaker's" job and give credit to this contribution to the family economy. This has been previously described in some detail.

This becomes important in *your* family only if you can illustrate to your children the lifestyle of *your* parents. This, ideally, includes work life, social life, and recreation. Try to illustrate it in a way that will show the parts of life that were better as well as those we are glad to have left behind.

When done with flair and good humor, this can be an enlightening experience. We have found that it is greatly enjoyed by preteens, teenagers, and even those older. Some illustrations seem quaint, some seem burdensome, and some truly heroic.

Your family will undoubtedly have an equally wide range of examples. In today's world of rapid change, these illustrations could be very dramatic and offer great learning experiences.

HISTORICAL THEME OF 1776

In 1976 we wished to share in the two-hundred year celebration. There was talk of the way our Constitution was written and agreed to as well as other "founding episodes." If your family would profit by a good understanding of the happenings, the movie *1776* is a great way to entertain and educate reference the history of our nation's founding. Available from our website.

In addition, several pioneer crafts were demonstrated. The variety of crafts that were shown included:

- Dying yarn naturally.

- Making handmade soaps with a bar on a pewter soap dish as a memento.

- Growing "broom corn" with a fourteen-foot stalk on display.

- Stamp collections of Early American stamps—with explanations of each.

Poetry Theme

One brave Chair Family chose "Share Your Favorite Poetry" for an annual theme. Much freedom was given, but *all* were encouraged to bring, read, or recite from memory their favorites. The choice of a favorite poem was, of course, indicative of feelings and values. The effort some put into preparation also indicated the value they placed on the Gathering.

Most of second-generation members had memorized much during school years. Many had developed a deep love for poetry. This also generated some fond memory and interesting stories, as it had been much of the second generation's entertainment during their "growing up" years on the farm.

Many of the third generation read or recited poetry—not usually as extensively as their parents.

However, an older member from California unable to travel sent "The Bridge Builder" by Will Allen Dromgoole. As it was read by his sister, it became apparent to all that for much of his life he had literally been "a traveler, traveling a lone highway." He had built many a bridge for the crossing that "to this fair haired youth, may a pitfall be." I am not sure that there was a dry eye left in the group

One of my sisters, after refreshing her memory, recited the entire twenty-nine stanzas, all 116 lines of

"Kentucky Belle." Again...the emotions that welled up in the group, the feelings of love and compassion, could not have been staged or planned for. What a blessing. Each member of the family got into the mood and made a valuable and significant contribution. This was an unexpected highlight.

COUNTY FAIR

It seemed that a universal experience of our extended family was the County Fair. Most of the family lived in small mid-western towns. Even those from other geographic areas also had vivid memories. Best of all each generation had experiences to share that were unique to that generation.

A not-so-fond memory:
One second-generation boy (me), a 4-H member, had a beef calf to show. It was customary for the owner to remain overnight. The local tradition was for upper classman to cut the freshman's hair to a half inch in length—not popular in that era. Needless to say when all was quiet at night, the deed was performed—with old-fashioned handheld sheep shears. Even with a couple of nicks in the scalp, there was no thought of legal action. Thankfully it was a less litigious time! (But it did smart a bit while it was happening.)

All second-generation members remember the County Fair as a great celebration. It was a week of opportunity to see a midway with rides, shows, and games of skill and/or chance. For all ages, it was a time to see friends from the entire county.

YOUR FAVORITE TOOL (ANOTHER SURPRISE THEME HIT!)

The theme, which seemed so strange when first mentioned, turned out to be full of interesting, helpful ideas and surprises.

Everyone first learned that a "trake" was a combination of trowel and rake. This was a favorite of, and highly recommended by, our Professional Gardener.

Others varied from a "Strong-arm" can opener, the all-purpose "Leatherman" tool, a favorite pocket knife, and the commercial tool by the President of the Company that manufactures it. There were a number of other interesting combinations of tools and users.

QUENCHING YOUR THIRST FOR KNOWLEDGE

What a myriad of interesting reports! An infinite variety is possible and many were shared. It seemed that most were drawn to inventions, travel, museums, books, back to school, new crafts, improving existing skills, new recreation, etc.

Family values showed so obviously here. These values, like many other important things in life, are more "caught" than "taught." This provided a vehicle to view many possibilities where teaching was inevitable without any "preaching" required.

FAVORITE AUTHOR OR BOOK

This turned out to be a surprising way for each member of the family to share their "gut level" values without seeming pushy or threatening.

It was an opportunity to see what each generation and each individual was deeply interested in. Several of the young were heavily into sports, who-done-it, or adventures. Several were into skills and management, and others were more interested in deeper reading.

Some especially meaningful discussions were initiated by the second generation or older third generation who shared how their interests had changed through the years. Often they moved from very light and easy reading to business and professional skills, and then usually to family values, life, and culture. Some broadened into religious and philosophical literature.

SUNDAY FAMILY SERVICE

Stemming from the influence outlined previously, the first and second generations were devout Christians. For the most part, in-laws and third and fourth generation family members have continued to be a part of this faith.

It was natural for the family to attend Sunday service in the home church when on the Farm. Later we attended outdoor summer services or visited a local church.

However, twenty years or more ago, it seemed natural to conduct our own service. There were enough with musical talent, speaking skills, etc., to have a complete and very personal experience. The host family runs the service and provides the speakers. Even though one member became an Ordained Minster after retirement and is very capable, all seem to value the personal and varied messages given by a member the host family chooses.

This varies widely, as we feel it should, since faith experience differs. It seems well distributed between the second and third generation. Some speakers have given personal testimonies in support of their faith in very personal and difficult times. Some have used lessons from Scripture or religious books. Some have taken examples from their experiences and deeply held beliefs.

In all cases, those who speak feel humbled in speaking before an audience that knows them so well. No chance or need for pretense. No one ever had a more favorable or responsive audience.

A manuscript and an audio book of one such message complete with details are included in the Reunion Planning Toolkit, Resource Pages. It is a family-oriented message suitable for most situations. While it may be useful, and you are free to use it any way you like, it is intended only as an example.

SUMMARY

Take care to be sure that the program includes something of interest for all and enough of the familiar to be comfortable. Also, plan enough new activities to keep interest and avoid boredom. Remember the 80/20 rule: 80% familiar activities and 20% new activities produces an enjoyable time for all.

The activities need to be easily understood and explained quickly and clearly so all feel certain of the role they are to play. Most activities need to be familiar.

A special something to highlight and give recognition to the younger generation is important. It has good inter-generational effect by giving the adults some special connection to discuss with each of the youth. Effort needs to be made to make the most of it.

Annual themes have added excitement to our family reunion. Do not overlook this possibility.

Keys to Secret Five:

1) Utilize active events of interest to each age group.

2) Use short family stories to build understanding and pride.

3) Select annual themes to both entertain and educate.

4) Include the family-faith journey.

CULTURAL FOCUS AND FAMILY RELATIONS

Secret Number Six:
Focus on the culture you want to encourage.

> If you would be loved, love and be lovable.
>
> Poor Richard's Almanac

Dear Amy,

Help! The holidays are approaching and I don't think I can make it another year with my in-laws. The environment is toxic and downright hostile. I am sick of being put down, disrespected and gossiped about by these bullies.

My husband says he has a thick skin and can take it, but I can't, and I can't stand the fact that my children are in this environment. The more we stand up to them, the more hostile they become.

Should I not bother with these people anymore?

I always felt that you should stand by your family, no matter what, but now I think that maybe this is not always true.

-Frustrated in the Northeast

In nearly every chapter some reference is made to the need for keeping a positive atmosphere. Some have questioned if this was overdone. This real "Dear Amy" question, plus talking to many others, illustrates to us the need to give conscious effort to promoting warm, caring relationships.

GROWTH OF FAMILY CULTURE

Many attitudes develop in every family without conscious effort. Each of us responds to the pressures and trials of life most often by the habits we formed in our early years.

Since the family as a whole is affected by these same happenings, the family develops a somewhat unified reaction. Although individuals will be different, the common thread that moves the group influences all.

From these happenings, be they war, untimely death, economic disaster, or an unexpected windfall, together with the attitude of the family leaders, cultural norms are formed. For the most part, we as a people are comfortable with our culture and tend to continue it, often without planning or thought.

USE REUNION TIME TO FOCUS

The Family Reunion planning is a good time to consciously consider the make-up of your group and the likely results of the influence your present family culture will have on future generations. Are there some influences that are destructive? Every family has both good and bad influences. An honest evaluation will allow emphasis on the part that will strengthen your family.

It is our belief that it strengthens each member to be aware of the strong influences of the family culture from our childhood. We believe also that at appropriate times, the weak points should be identified—though not dwelt upon.

Transparency and honesty of our forbearers seem to be the best policy. You will recall the "Family Tree" painting of America's beloved Norman Rockwell. It clearly shows pirates and horse thieves, as well as the elite of society. It is reasonable to assume that this represents most of our families and indeed life itself.

This provides a wonderful opportunity to be factual and realistic, yet still illustrates that we are each responsible for our own destiny. Usually, we can find heroic examples of family members who have overcome great difficulty to make great contributions.

On occasions, we may have a family example to illustrate the recent book by Dr. Laura Schlesinger, *Bad Childhood, Good Life* (available from (www.successfulfamilyreunions. org). This should leave no room for excuses but can show understanding of any difficulty.

THE POWER OF FAMILY CULTURE

My daughter rushed to the grocery store for a few last minute items before leaving for the family reunion. In her enthusiasm she mentioned this to the sixty-something lady in the checkout line in front of her. Responding to questions she mentioned "900 miles each way to see sixty to sixty-five family members."

Tears filled her new friend's eyes. "I have more family members than that within a fifty-mile radius. I could not get even one of them to visit my mother while she was dying in the hospital for two weeks. A few did come to her funeral.

What I would give for a family like yours!"

A Public and Well-Known Example of Family Culture

Most readers of this will recall the heart wrenching scene of *The Sound of Music* when Georg Von Trap comes from a meeting in Vienna with the Nazis and says to Maria, "we must decide—do we keep our material wealth and give up our spiritual heritage, or do we keep our spiritual heritage and give up our material wealth?" This decision, of course, caused them to abandon all their material possessions while escaping from their homeland, which was at that time overrun by the Nazi hordes. Eventually they come to America with little but their clothes.

An Example We Found in Our Family History

Through a long ago conversation with a Great Uncle, confirmed by recent research, I found a similar, but not such a dramatic happening, in our own family. My siblings and I had often wondered how our Grandparents came to settle in Southern Indiana, where they became prosperous farmers with large barns, cattle, horses, and enough land to give sixty to seventy acres of land to each of eight children. This size farm was unusual in an era where all farming was done with horses and manual labor.

The following facts were gleaned with reference to our maternal Grandmother, whose name was Robertson. She was one of eight children.

Bill and Hellen Robertson, with eight children, were living in Kentucky at the time of the Civil War. Lines were sharply drawn. Kentucky was known as a "border state" and tolerant of slavery.

They decided they did not want their children to grow up with that cultural influence. This was important enough that they chose to move the family some two hundred miles to an unknown place in Indiana. To a free state where slavery was illegal.

We were not able to determine the exact extent of the sacrifice, but those of us who have moved, even in this modern age, know it to be substantial.

Historical records show that Billy Robertson gave the land for the local Methodist Church. He, with two others, built the church that has been so influential in the life of this family.

This was used as a part of a Sunday Sermon at a recent Family Reunion.

Teach Future Generations from Bad Examples

(Most Families Have These Examples Too)

With such a heritage, one might assume such values would be transmitted to all future generations through natural events. The truth is not so tidy.

My mother, the Matriarch of our clan, was the grandchild of Billy and Hellen Robertson. She, at every appropriate occasion, reminded us of the need for family siblings to be open, caring, and above all recognizing that material possessions were not important enough to sacrifice a family relationship.

She convinced each of her seven children of that fact. Often the younger generations marveled at our spirited exchanges with strongly held opinions, which never resulted in hard feelings, grudges, or concerns beyond the moment.

Contrast that with two of her eight siblings—all grandchildren of Billy and Hellen Robertson. One aunt, our closest neighbor to our west, and one uncle, our closest neighbor to our east, spent more than twenty-five years (until the uncle's death) without speaking to each other—even when rural living brought them in close proximity.

Although details were never discussed, and rarely mentioned, the best-known facts went something like this:

Near the end of my grandfather's life, he willed the farm to his children, giving each sixty to seventy acres. Of course, as one farm, all wagon roads had been open. After ownership passed, one chose to install a gate with a lock—perfectly legal. The other, after a hard day's work, was surprised to find it locked. Rather than take a longer way home, he gained access by use of an axe from the standard work tools in his wagon.

One felt that the road that had once been open should always be open. The other felt that since they now had legal possession to the property, they should deny access to assert those rights. With neither willing to compromise, animosity blossomed. The pain and suffering of that family, the community, and future generations was obvious to everyone—except the two siblings involved.

As Robert Frost made famous, "Good fences make good neighbors." After witnessing the effect of such poor judgment, my mother spent her life's effort teaching her children to use better judgment.

A classic example of the wizards answer proves truthful. When asked, "To what do you attribute your good judgment?" the wizard replied, "Learning from my bad judgment." Hopefully, we can learn from other's bad judgment as well.

Our Family Culture

In our own situation, we were very much a working class family. We were farm raised in the Midwest, where economic recovery was slow. This affected everything we did as well as our attitudes.

- The land was a sacred trust, and we were obligated to be good stewards.

- Animals were to be well treated and cared for—but not given human status.

- Work ethic was strong; we were proud to earn our bread by the "sweat of our brow."

- Our basic attitude was that we could accomplish whatever we set our mind to. We believed that "problems yield to human effort."

- Teamwork was expected and the value of it was so obvious, it needed no explanation.

Responsibility for a specific task was assigned and accepted at a very early age. Such jobs as gathering eggs and stocking the house with kindling and firewood were jobs that, if omitted, got an immediate response. Unreasonable jobs were never assigned. Our mother had the ability and patience to develop in each of us a feeling of ownership and pride in being a productive member of the team.

We have tried to include such training in our own families. The second generation found it required intentional planning. This has served us well in planning our family reunion. We find a great willingness for all to join in the effort required. Each family takes their turn being the host family—creating, planning, and executing. But when extra hands are needed, all are readily available—usually without asking.

The culture of openness and frankness that developed as the second generation grew up together has also been a blessing. We hope it has been instructive to our future generations.

Decision-Making Process

In the early days of developing the pattern of our reunion, many basic decisions were made. It was essential to have a free exchange and the ability to come to acceptable decisions. Such decisions as date and length of the gathering, location, food, activities, and a myriad of smaller details need to be easily resolved without lingering conflict. To do it well a frank exchange is necessary and, in our case, was inevitable.

We were happy to find that the stressful conditions natural to the early environment of the second generation helped us develop most of these traits. It also provided the flexibility that was useful.

Many years later, we learned that team-building training in business and industry often centers on a well-defined task performed in an artificially created stressful environment. Perhaps it was a blessing that we had real stress; we certainly needed no *artificial* stress added to our environment.

Bird's Eye View of Our Second-Generation Families

The second generation found they had to be even more intentional to develop these qualities in their offspring. Each of the family groups found different ways of meeting their individual needs in their particular situations.

- Three formed businesses that allowed some assignment of responsibilities that were suitable and could be adjusted to the age and maturity level of the growing children.

- One had a Garden Farm homestead that provided opportunity for proper assignments of responsibility and follow-up for five growing children.

- One had a large garden and an extensive lake property that was useful (and used) to accomplish the same level of training and development that is useful in developing confidence and responsibility.

- In our own situation, where I labored in the manufacturing management of a major American chemical company, it seemed more difficult. The constant moves, usually at inappropriate times, made extended and growing responsibilities more difficult to assign. However, intentional effort was made wherever there was an opportunity. In addition, vacations were planned with those needs in mind. A wide variety of trips, requiring each individual to assume a suitable responsibility, was a maturing experience for all concerned, although it was not always realized or appreciated by our three children at the time.

EXAMPLES OF ONE FAMILY

Appreciation of the learning our children experienced became obvious decades later, at the celebration of a big birthday of mine, when our children referred to the confidence, ability, and resourcefulness learned through our summer holiday trips. Items mentioned were:

A) A one-week bicycle tour of Pennsylvania's Amish Country.

B) Two weeks backpacking through Isle Royale National Park.

C) Extensive hiking in the Olympia State Park in Washington State.

D) A wide variety of wilderness trips in the Southern Appalachians

E) Car camping under canvas at night—from coast to coast

These generated both sufficient team needs and sufficient stress!

Even as the second generation is gradually passing the baton to the third generation, the pattern of freedom of the host (Annual Chair Family) seems to be continuing. No one seems to have the feeling that the family reunion is an entitlement but a deserved result of community effort.

Decision making still seems to work best with the blood relatives taking the most active public role. Time is given for the in-laws' views to be amply discussed in more private conversations. Also, major controversies cross over and are resolved at the highest generational level practical with continued freedom of expression and understanding.

YOUR FAMILY CULTURE

These examples illustrate the development of our families' culture at both the First/Second generation and at the Second/Third generation levels.

To be successful at this part of the process of building a Successful Family Reunion, *you must identify what is important to your family.* You must decide what parts of your family culture that you want to support and then be sure that you pass them on.

It is very gratifying to see this growth take shape

Take time to determine what family traditions you want to promote and pass on to the next generations. Intentionally decide on some that will add strength and stability to the families of the future. The book titled *Family Traditions* by Leadbetter and Smith will be helpful to you (available from www.successfulfamilyreunions.org).

GO FOR WHAT YOU WANT YOUR FAMILY TO BECOME

What was Dear Amy's answer?

We like her answer, but would prefer to prevent this situation before it starts.

> Dear Frustrated: So far, your in-laws think that they can say anything without consequences, so this holiday season, give them the gift that keeps on giving.

> Consequences.

> Your husband's ability to withstand and absorb abuse isn't a quality that you want your children to witness or imitate. You should either completely minimize the contact with these people, or consider cutting out contact altogether this holiday season and turn your attention to your own family—building fun experiences together.

Keys to Secret Six:

1) Recognize and develop the family culture.

2) Demonstrate culture intentionally.

3) Make it fun for the kids of the family to take an active part in learning your family culture.

Strategic Planning

Secret Number Seven:
Continuing reunions need to plan for leadership change.

> The will to succeed is important, but what's even more important is the will to prepare.
>
> Bobby Knight

Have you ever heard someone say, "We used to have Family Reunions, but…," "Alice and Bill used to plan our Family Reunion, but they don't want to do it anymore," or something like, "The Younger generation has lost interest"?

These are common complaints—but it doesn't need to be that way. However…careful planning is required

Planning Makes It Happen

It is a great accomplishment to have any significant family reunion.

We believe those planning a reunion will be well served to go into the first one with some thought of how to keep it happening again and again.

You probably *do not* want to tell everyone that this is going to go on annually before the first one has been successful. There is no doubt that the major rewards of family bonding and other things discussed in this book will only be realized if reunions are continuous.

Our experience has mostly been with our own annual meeting for the last forty years. Prior to that, we met on two to five-year intervals. We have heard of those who get together every five years, some every two years, and we know of one family who has the older generation meet alone on odd-numbered years while all join together on even-numbered years.

Need to Think Ahead

I feel strongly that meetings annually are best by far. We know that any family reunion is better than none. Everyone must find the best regular schedule possible for their individual family. Annual gatherings over any period of years require more planning then meets the eye.

We were fortunate that a sudden realization of the need to actively plan ahead came without a family trauma. In the first six to eight years, activities moved along with great fun and enthusiasm. All enjoyed the vigor of our ages and the excitement of competitive games during the afternoon "game time."

After one particularity ongoing tug-of-war, my older sister severely scolded me, reminding me that my brother was fifteen years older and had a weak heart. The sudden realization of the disaster that could result in such a situation was quietly discussed and was the beginning of much more careful and strategic planning of activities.

Key Factors in Planning

Just by looking around, we could see that a few of the third generation had married and was beginning to bring spouses. It was equally apparent that others were on the verge of marrying and that a new era was about to dawn.

A brief conversation among the second generation, my siblings (hoping to be as clear as possible) indicated a change in activities would be useful. Less strenuous games were scheduled for adults.

The New-Child Effect

With a new generation growing and becoming more active, we felt the need for an evening activity that would include all ages. A Saturday evening square-dance caller was found. The change in the program had the desired effect. The involvement of the young couples and the informal atmosphere was a hit.

We have found that a highly accomplished square dance caller is not required. Someone who knows the entry level, simple dances is perfectly adequate. What is important is that the caller is personable, flexible, and accomplished at teaching fundamentals. It is helpful if the caller's spouse comes along and can assist in demonstration.

It is quite predictable that two to four years after a "rash" of marriages, there will be an increase in the family population. Those new parents will be too busy in the early evening for a Square Dance.

At this point, evenings of reviewing some pictures of early reunions or some other quiet activity was called for. Most of the group stayed involved. Pictures of such things as wedding receptions, the Farm, a good mix of vacations, family history, or similar events have worked well. Family slideshows always generate some good-natured fun at how we all looked "back then."

Soon, as families grew, a Saturday evening hayride included all ages and kept the interest of the group. This included parents with babes in arms as well as older children. It kept all active and was a nice change of pace. It allowed additional time for visiting and reviewing pictures, scrapbooks, etc., by the more sedentary members of the family.

It is amazing how quickly the flock of young children became active enough for the Square Dance to resume. The young love to be involved with youth and family members, and everyone enjoys the social aspect of this activity, which includes all generations.

This is also a time when a new activity can be introduced. A family historical documentary, indoor games, or crafts of general interest can be introduced. It is difficult, however, to have these activities be of sufficient interest for all age groups. This is essential to have it be successful. Be careful. Newlyweds need to be incorporated into things they enjoy.

OTHER PLANNING FACTORS

This generational change of marriage, children, busy parents, growing children, marriage, and aging is inevitable. It needs to be the major factor in strategic planning. It is *very* important to give it thought and be leading the curve instead of reacting to complaints.

Yet everyone doesn't fall within the main curve and some generations will have two populations to consider. However, any consideration and intentional planning with flexibility is far better than a hard and fast repetitive agenda.

We, the second generation, spent our childhood attending Sunday basket dinners and a one to one and a half-hour program, largely a historical family history lecture by a well-known family member, who was a local Judge. We were told that "we should listen and be a part of it."

No attempt was made at showing interest in us, and there were no intellectual activities for family bonding. This system worked well for one generation, but our generation participated as adults, largely, to please our parents and did not continue the reunion as the older generation left the scene.

Strategic planning is essential to keep long-term viability of any arrangements or function. Meeting the needs or desires of the "customer" is necessary. Building the interest of coming generations is the goal.

The generational changes are the most obvious and the easiest to respond to. There are, however, many more subtle elements. Location can be an attraction. Just as the family is in constant change, the facilities at any given location are also in flux.

It is important to continually ask: Does it still meet our needs? Does it add to or detract from the reunion's main goal? Has the price gotten too high to be sustainable? Does it fit all ages and interests in the "free time" allotted? Has its attractions changed enough to become distractions to our objectives of building new relationships and strengthening existing ones?

Each family may have different answers—which is as it should be. As long as leaders continue to consider this, the correct answers will surface.

EVIDENCE OF SUCCESS

On the occasion of getting serious with his current girlfriend one nephew said to his mom, "Don't worry, Mom, the girl I marry will need to enjoy the family reunion, for I'm going to be there!"

Fortunately after her attendance for two years, all seems well!

THEME OF THE YEAR

We have found that some specific focus is helpful in deepening our knowledge and understanding of one another. Values show and they are important. Selecting a theme of the year is a way to have an exchange between generations in a non-threatening manner.

We are always surprised at the wide variety of expressions a theme will simulate. Some are generational; some seem to be common to a certain nuclear family. Some are off-the-wall, which can come as a surprise to close family members as well as to the general extended family.

Several themes were reflected in chapter five. These same themes, or similar ones that work well, can be repeated with only a few years between. Thought should be given to themes that will encourage, but not force, an ever-deepening level of sharing. If a high trust level exists, this will result in an ever increasing strengthening of family bonds.

Recognition—To Include All

Many years ago Dale Carnegie stated the fact that we all need recognition as a major principle in *How to Win Friend and Influence People*. This has become a classic and is still the foundation of widely recognized seminars. This is a fundamental lesson in all sales instruction. We ignore this fact at our peril.

In my generation's experience, referred to earlier, we had to be "seen and not heard." When we had the option to avoid those meetings, we opted out. At our own reunion, early on each nuclear family had a specific time after a meal to respond to the theme, hit the highlights of the previous year, and touch on the year to come. Most adults participated.

It was noticed that young children and some youth drifted away to gather outside to play or chat. They were neither hearing nor being heard. We decided to set aside the Sunday after-dinner segment for the fourth generation. This was our last full meal, and most formal occasion with every family member present. This became, for each of that generation—some of whom were very young—a short, formal talk to sixty-plus people.

It is universally understood that a major fear of Americans is "speaking in public." This, of course, caused—and still causes—some trepidation among children and parents in preparing. However, it is invariably reported by parents that the children feel "nine feet tall" when they have successfully completed their presentation. It is incumbent upon the audience to see that each speaker has a successful experience. Generous applause, favorable comments, and relevant questioning afterward is all an important part of this success.

It also gives the parents an opportunity for coaching and becoming a helpful associate to the child in a meaningful way. The speakers, of course, can be assured they will never have a more understanding and appreciative audience. It is great to witness the maturity developing among the next generations.

Here is one recent example, which I happened to be in the right location to observe.

The youngest member of a family had just turned eight years old. He strode manfully to the podium and, without regard to the microphone, articulated clearly a couple of events he enjoyed last year. He told one item he was looking forward to in the coming year. During this entire time his eyes were only on his dad, who sat on the center aisle in the next to the last row. When the applause started, he was in his dad's arms in a flash. It was apparent that father and son had made and felt a great accomplishment.

ADDITIONAL CONSIDERATIONS

The above have been major steps in our family planning. There are other items that merit consideration.

1) Sharing the burden and pleasure of Leadership.

2) Overall cost of the activity. We must be aware of travel, food, and lodging as being a burden to some, especially the young families, etc.

3) Do the activities at the venue distract from the family time?

4) Food quality. Is it possible to supplement with picnic-type lunches, salads, Continental breakfasts, etc.?

5) Dates that encourage maximum attendance.

6) Ways to continually see that the youth *enjoy* the experience. Apply the rule learned in scouting. Remind the Scouts of the fun goals, remind the parents of the character-building goals. Use both fun and family values.

However, the most important key to strategic planning is to *recognize the need!*

Keys to Secret Seven:

1) Consider altering activities needed to meet changing family size, age, and interest.

2) Project expected changes in facilities.

3) Be sure the younger generations are involved.

Pitfalls to Avoid

Secret Number Eight:
Minimize adverse consequences by careful planning.

> Always keep an open mind and a compassionate heart.
>
> Phil Jackson

In our world of media sound bytes, I should have expected this question…I get it all the time.

Question: Uncle Bob, you talk about all these years of Family reunions, but I just want to know…what one thing will guarantee success?

Answer: I'm not sure there is only one thing that will guarantee a successful reunion under all conditions.

- There is one thing that ranks above all others.

- It will change a mediocre event to a great one and make most any event a good one.

- It will build a strong desire to return in the future.

Create and maintain a positive atmosphere throughout the entire event!

SIMPLE AND EASY?

If that sounds simple, it is. But like many simple things, not as easy as it sounds.

First, just rethink how much negative stuff is out there:

- Any newspaper headline
- Any TV news report
- Any talk show
- Your work situation
- Sports

If it is bad for adults, think what our kids live with:

- Shootings in school
- Sex in the sixth grade
- Verbal harassment from a competitive group
- Trash talk from jealous classmates
- Pressure from gangs

How long has it been since you have spent a week or a long weekend in a warm, positive atmosphere? *Have your kids ever done this?*

FAILURE TO ESTABLISH GOALS

Having established and well-understood goals is important to the planning process. We have mentioned earlier how this acts as a guide to those planning programs and activities.

Goals give direction to the youth games for team-building exercises. They give direction to the overall program to encourage sharing of family legacy to give members a sense of "belonging to the club." They also give direction to themes to encourage sharing of values and to promote better understanding among members.

Authority to Set Standards

Some have said, "Everyone knows what we think is important," or "We don't need formal goals." It is not necessary to take a vote if it is well understood that building positive relationships, creating a strong support group, or developing a sense of belonging is the priority.

This gives authority when someone is pushing an agenda that detracts from the planner's intent.

A well-established goal gives authority when someone becomes belligerent. This could be the result of a marriage failure, depression, alcohol overload, etc. It gives the planner, usually together with other leaders, authority to explain the effect of the member's action and solicit a change in attitude. In the worst case, an invitation could be withdrawn.

A goal also gives authority to limit the invitations to certain family groups. This is not meant to limit individuals, except as mentioned in the above paragraph, but to decide on the branches of the family that have agreed to like goals and have like interests.

When any of these things need attention, a quick discussion with recognized leaders will usually find that the concerns are commonly shared. This gives a small group the moral authority to understand the level of disruption and reach agreement on the need for a change in attitude or action.

Regardless of how much careful planning occurs, there is always the possibility of adverse consequences occurring. Better to have considered these than to be caught off guard. Simple items such as inclement weather, late arrivals, etc., can be worked around or taken in stride—as adverse consequences are recognized, plans can be made to avoid them or to lesson their effects.

It is easy to give too much emphasis to things that could go wrong. That is often the cause of delaying or avoiding entirely the idea of a family reunion. *Don't let this happen!*

Do not hesitate to schedule a planning discussion, with appropriate family leaders and get started. Be carefully observant with the thought of minimizing any negative effects and emphasizing the positive aspects. Most will tend to give planners the benefit of any doubt.

However, it seems good to identify some things we have learned from experience.

Remember that families vary.

Avoid Outdated Models

Nothing can be more certain to kill interest than trying blindly to repeat the pattern of past generations. In my growing-up years, it was quite standard to have the third Sunday in August set aside for the family to meet at the local park. The adults renewed acquaintance, the children enjoyed running wild, and teenagers complained, vowing to never come to another family reunion.

This worked reasonably well for the farm-based families who arrived from churches with full baskets of fried chicken, farm-fresh vegetables, salads, and wide selections of the best pies you will ever eat.

Families had one car. They came and went together. The milking needed to be done on time. All hands were needed, at home, around 5 p.m. Five to six hours was ample time for the women to inspect the new babies and advise the young mothers. The men had exchanged on crops and weather, and together had solved the world's problems. The reunion was a success.

NEW EXPECTATIONS

In today's world, adults have greater expectations for a family reunion. More importantly teenagers have their own wheels or access to friends who have cars. They have something to do, although it is often unclear exactly what it is. To have continuity through the generations, a different model is required.

Nearly as disastrous as the old standard model is to build around a specific age or interest group. This may work well for a large portion of the group. However, if the desire is to have the reunion continue through the generations, each group, and indeed each person, needs to have their place in the sun.

Universal Need for Affirmation

We need to face the fact that today's world is not centered on giving us affirmation, building up our self-confidence, or showing appreciation for our accomplishments. This is true for adults in the workplace and in our social interactions. This is even more pronounced and more destructive in the world of the teenager. All too often their world consists of bullying, putting people down, and stereotyping others in very negative ways.

It is not necessary to announce this as our goal. In fact, it may be counterproductive to do so. Just the same, we should recognize that to spend a long weekend together showing mutual respect, devoid of the negativism that rains down on our heads daily, is a real relief.

If you can give each an environment, even for this short time, that produces a positive influence, where each can be certain that they are valued, cared for, and respected, it will strike a responsive cord. If a trust level can be developed where each feels free to tell of their accomplishments in an open, caring environment, they will be firmly committed.

Venue Must Have Something for All

If the venue selected does not meet the needs of all, this will have a strong detrimental effect.

One important way it should meet the needs is to be in a suitable price range. There is often substantial variation in the amount of discretionary income among family groups. Consideration needs to be given to see that no one is excluded for financial reasons. This, of course, does not preclude close family members from giving support to a young starting family or some one with a temporary set-back. This can happen for any myriad of reasons.

If a family-owned site (home or farm location) is suitable, that can reduce costs. State parks are often inexpensive and usually have a variety of accommodations allowing a broad price range—lodges, cabins, camping. This was dealt with in more detail in chapter three.

Avoid Narrow Leadership

Avoid too much reliance on what might be considered elite, senior leadership. This may be the capable planning group that was responsible for the initial gathering. Even then, the program will lack the freshness that comes from different planning groups. It also reduces ownership and creates the feeling that it is "their" reunion—not ours.

As soon as possible, a formal way of passing leadership should be devised, with flexibility to provide the sometimes necessary, although unexpected, changes.

Similarly, and important enough to warrant addressing it openly, is the need to keep the occasion from becoming boring. All parents have learned that youth responds well to challenges but dies of boredom. Adults may be more patient and polite, but the gut level reaction is the same.

Passing planning responsibilities around, as mentioned in chapter four, is a good approach. It is important for all to recognize that each annual event should have some of the new, for interest and excitement; also, some of the old for comfort.

Failure to Intentionally Build Bonding Activities

Failure to build bonding or relational activities into the reunion can result in having it not seem worthwhile. The world we live in on an everyday basis can be extremely negative. Just to be involved for a whole weekend with friendly family members with whom we have much in common adds a very positive factor to life.

"I can live for a week on one compliment," is a statement attributed to Mark Twain. Regardless of who said it, we universally acknowledge its validity. Think of the effect you feel as an individual expresses appreciation for your accomplishments. It helps, even more, to feel the warmth and acceptance of your entire extended family. Added to that is good-natured fun.

You may say this is too much to expect or too difficult. We have found that where families generally care for each other, this atmosphere shows. It can easily be enhanced with some intentional thought and planning.

We have not used the "mixer" techniques that are standard and effective in Stranger Groups. To us that would seem contrived and artificial. Providing an opportunity for each to share something personal, at the intimacy level they choose, in an atmosphere of trust has been effective. In addition, we need activities on a continuing basis to draw all participants to a "return engagement."

Each person needs to leave each reunion looking forward to a return for some specific reason. Adults may have had a discussion reference the coming year with family members and look forward to a return discussion or review. Youth and children are more likely to respond to competitive activity, especially those that occur only at the reunion.

Such activities as egg toss, stilts, and puzzles can be experienced year after year without growing old.

Avoid Being Too Repetitious

Avoid repeating the same program without variation. Even if one year just seems to "click" extremely well, review the reasons, but don't try to repeat it verbatim.

Include Family Comfort Food

Food is one of the more sensitive issues and will be somewhat different for each family. This is one of the more expensive items—competing with housing for the most expensive item. It is also one of the more controversial. Nearly everyone is conscious of gaining a few pounds on any weekend. And, of course, there is a celebration aspect of such a weekend.

Initially we solved this by doing much of our own cooking. With planning and group involvement it afforded much interaction and pleasure. It also allowed us to indulge in some "comfort food" represented by the well-loved recipes from the Farm. Such items as the famous persimmon pudding—brought from home.

Another highlight occurred the year one family arrived with a camp trailer that included a Coleman stove. Another arrived with dried apples, flour, sugar, etc. The twenty-five dried apple, fried apple, half-moon pies "just like Mother used to make" was devoured with relish.

More recent times, simpler food has been served, and more food delivered or brought in by a caterer. Still in this family, fruit, granola, and rolls make a preferred breakfast. The favorite Saturday lunch includes the specialty salads of each family, with the anticipated three fruit cobblers from the kitchen of three senior bakers.

It is important to watch carefully the enthusiasm for various plans; solicit input from the mothers who get the feedback and keep the system flexible.

Give Careful Attention to the Drink Table

Perhaps the most controversial of all decisions is the question of drinks. It is very important to have ample coffee, tea, water, and a selection of cold drinks from the Friday Eve "gathering period" through to the final Sunday Meal and also between meals, at the games, and for snacks. It is especially important to have plenty of cold, wholesome drinks on a hot day. This encourages good conversation, sometimes in small groups or sometimes one on one, which is the heart of the exchange.

Even more important is how you choose to deal with alcoholic beverages. This is very dependent upon the culture of the family. However, it is very important to have a policy that is understood and agreed upon.

Our family, as most, consists of some teetotalers and some who are not. However, it is recognized that where alcoholic beverages become a part of a picnic celebration, at least one or two will overdo. This reduces logical discussion and rational exchange, thereby defeating much of our purpose.

We have chosen to have no alcoholic beverages as a regular part of our activity. Undoubtedly some have a nightcap before turning in. We are delighted that during our forty consecutive years of experience, alcohol has been avoided in our activities and has not been a problem. We believe this is a particularly good policy where families of all ages are included and much freedom is allowed.

Keys to Secret Eight:

1) Keep leadership broad based and intentional.

2) Include bonding and recognition opportunities

3) Consider carefully the effect of food and drink.

UNUSUAL REUNIONS-SPECIALTY FOCUS

Secret Number Nine:
Creativity in special situations brings new dimensions to the family.

> Belief in a thing makes it happen.
>
> Frank Lloyd Wright

Question: *You continually recommend keeping reunions simple, serving picnic style food, and hosting it at State Parks. Can't we have an even better reunion in a more comfortable setting?*

Answer: *If that is the message you heard, we didn't make our point. It is not about money. It is about having everyone present, keeping a positive atmosphere, and telling the family story, including values and history.*

Any reunion that does this well—making life more meaningful—will give a better understanding to our youth and add stability to our families. Future generations will thank you for it.

No "One Size Fits All" Model

Our model, as described in earlier chapters, will not suit all families. Human nature and extended families are much too varied for this. Therefore, we suggest other models be considered.

We encourage you to find a model that fits your family situation and launch a plan to start your family on the road to mutual respect, cultural understanding, and togetherness.

From my own experience and research of how other families have had successful family reunions, I will offer these suggestions to fit all reunions.

1. Be sure the date is well established approximately a year in advance. Having a fixed annual repeat date is good.

2. Get a written "save the date" notice to all approximately eight to ten months in advance. Include a special reason for attending this year.

3. A notice three months in advance and then a last-minute notice approximately two weeks in advance.

4. Plan a well-organized program that allows for some flexibility and fits the needs of all ages. Teenagers are the most difficult to keep interested. Have something special for them, to give them recognition for accomplishment.

5. Be sure everyone leaves with the feeling of a successful reunion and warm fellowship.

We offer the following models to stimulate your thinking. They have worked with great success for some families.

LARGE FAMILY REUNIONS

Several family reunions now attract family members in the hundreds. Some exceed 1,000 in attendance. This, of course, requires a different model than we have used. This requires different emphasis, different financial planning, and a different schedule of events.

These large reunions can be effective with more time between, usually three to five years. They also need to be formally organized with a well defined decision-making process. Smaller regional or family segments often meet during the off years.

See chapter five for more details. Even more information is available at www.successfulfamilyreunions.org.

DO AFFLUENT FAMILIES NEED TO TEACH FAMILY VALUES?

Our newspapers are filled with families that have amassed great material wealth and failed to transmit family values to sustain it.

Roy Williams, head of the Williams Group, has studied more than 3,250 families to see how successfully their wealth is passed on. He concludes that only 30% of those who fail to successfully transmit their material possessions to the next generation do so because of poor accounting or legal advice. The larger group fails because of failure to transmit the proper culture and values.

It does not need to be so!

Venue Selection for the Affluent Family Gathering

Usually those with interest and ability to enjoy this type of reunion have traveled a great deal, are already familiar with suitable locations, or enjoy exploring those places that would give the family the experience they have in mind.

Certainly a visit to the internet via your favorite search engine will provide a list of resorts to meet your criteria with contact information. Also a visit to your favorite magazine will suggest contacts for the type of event you have in mind. Most such resorts have event planners to assist and are very responsive to Family Reunions.

The magazine *Reunions* contains the best information for reunions in general, while specializing in family reunions. It suggests a wide variety of venues at different economic levels as well as general assistance. A review of such national magazines as *Conte-Nast Traveler*, *Robb Report*, etc., will provide ample stimulation and contacts. All of these should be studied, both their content and their paid advertising. *Country Life* has a wide selection, plus an easy response form for seventy-five to one hundred interesting places.

There are many regional first-class magazines that contain this type information for their respective regions—*Yankee* for the East, *Midwest Living*, and *Southern Living* for their respective areas, and *Sunset* for the West.

Just select your goal and choose one that fits best.

FAMILY GATHERINGS OF THE AFFLUENT

One of the families of our second generation has been uncommonly successful in one lifetime. They have always participated in and enjoyed our forty-plus family member reunions.

In addition, these members have elected to do some unusual things with their nuclear family, which consists of two members of the first generation, three members of the second generation, and two third-generation children.

Through the years they have traveled extensively in the US. They enjoyed national, historical locations as well as special locations mostly in the western US. Here they can repeat the activities that they especially enjoy.

In addition they have planned international trips that allowed the entire family to accomplish much more than entertainment and sightseeing.

INTIMATE FAMILY IN EUROPE

One such trip was to Northern Italy where a villa was rented. This came complete with housekeeper, who advised on specifics of the region and assisted as interpreter to some degree.

This was carefully studied and planned. It afforded great insight into the local culture, the history of the area, its impact on their home nation, and the world around them.

This was great fun and of interest to the family. It was also mentally very stimulating. It was particularly advantageous for the two young children of the family.

Later, a similar trip was planned and completed to France. There was a short visit in a large city, but most of the time was spent in a smaller village where they could become closer to the local population and understand the culture better.

No doubt these will be memories to last a lifetime.

Examples for Related Families

We are aware that in some families, this could cause jealousy and resentment. However, this has not been evident.

Those of their generation have observed that this success was a result of unusual focus, dedication, and business acumen. To any of the younger generation who may not understand that, all have been anxious to point this out.

It is an unusual opportunity to illustrate to younger generations that each of us has greater capability than we use. This example also gives us the opportunity to support our belief that our nation, in spite of its shortcomings, is the best governing system known. No other nation offers such opportunity.

Explaining this has been made easier by the fact that, while this family has lived very comfortably, they have not indulged in the extravagant excesses that make headlines. As well as to their business, they have dedicated themselves to their church, family, and community in an uncommon way.

They have allowed us a good example to prove that Kipling was correct in his poem "If" when he taught that we could "meet with triumph or disaster, and treat those two imposters just the same."

A DIFFERENT AFFLUENT MODEL

Family friends of ours have chosen a different model for transmitting value to the third generation.

This family invites the grandchildren of appropriate age to a summer vacation (usually two weeks) that includes a preplanned European trip for in-depth learning and mind stretching as well as fun. Other family members are invited in order to manage and enjoy the trip.

The price to the grandchildren is to study an assigned segment of the trip, prepare a written summary, and give a presentation to the group. This is meant to entail significant study and provide a "resident expert" for the group on each major area of interest.

The presenter is to be prepared to answer questions at the presentations and also during the trip. Of course, even an in-depth study does not make one a native historian, but it does provide a source of knowledge to supplement the group; since each has a similar assignment, there is mutual sharing and good fellowship.

One recent trip was a flight to Athens for four days studying historical areas, and a few days on a three-mast sailing ship in the Mediterranean. The remainder of the two weeks was spent in Rome and Southern Italy.

The youth returned having had a wonderful experience that taught them to understand much more about how those important cultures have affected our world. Each had the experience of being "the expert" on a segment of the trip and had learned to seek information from "other experts" on points of interest.

We believe that family culture and values were incorporated into this important event.

Cruise Models

We know of several families who have traveled together with large family groups on cruises. Our understanding is that these are usually one-time trips and not given to annual or even frequent repetition. They tend to be interesting experiences, can be expensive, and require more time than many can spend away. They are not focused on transmitting culture and values.

Resorts for Family Reunions

There is much variation in resort facilities. Many plan activities for various age groups with supervision leaving adults to enjoy themselves. Many of these focus on pleasure and entertainment, both of which can be worthwhile goals.

Some resorts are said to be prepared to assist families in accomplishing their specific objectives; they certainly have the facilities and abilities to do so. It seems to us that these could be excellent, but would require much input and participation from family members to make them of meaningful, long-term value to family members.

Care may need to be taken to subsidize youth and young couples.

Church Retreats and Venues

Church retreats have a long history in our nation, having grown from the "camp meetings" of the 1800s to a wide variety of different types in various geographic areas in the US.

Some still retain the camping/RV emphasis while others have morphed into upscale resorts.

The most famous of these, no doubt, is Chautauqua, located in upstate New York. It started in 1874 as a Methodist Camp meeting and is now a village surrounded by a chain-link fence. It contains many private homes, many hotels, and some church-owned facilities.

There was a time, before television and the internet provided a national stage, when this was the largest and most diverse crowd that could be assembled. Presidents, presidential hopefuls, great theologians, and others wanting to influence the nation sought this stage. Theodore Roosevelt even, both prior to and during his presidency, spoke from that stage.

Some years ago, I had the pleasure of five mornings with Buckminster Fuller at this location. He was listed, without apology, as their "resident genius" for the week. As a Graduate Engineer with years of practice, three of his lectures were greatly enjoyed; two went completely over my head.

Chautauqua has its program nearly equally divided between exercise and athletics, cultural lectures and religious teaching, and arts and crafts. It is indeed an interesting place where children can have much freedom. It also offers a variety of stimulating experiences for adults. Their excellent and diverse library is a real joy for the readers in your family.

We have known at least three couples that have taken family groups to Church Retreats for a week. It always provides a unique opportunity and growing experience. These venues tend to have generational related programs with very busy schedules. This limits the amount of fellowship and bonding within the family. Done in addition to a family reunion, these make a wonderful vacation. We do not feel they are an adequate replacement for a family reunion.

Lake/Seaside Cottage

Most of us own or have family members or friends who own second homes on lakes or seashores. These are often great experiences for the nuclear family to enjoy wonderful times together. They usually become woven into the fabric of their relationship.

Even in the situations we know, where the nuclear family members own three homes in close proximity, it has not lent itself to large family reunions.

Often the geographic location is unsuitable, and sometimes they are small and lend themselves more to various individuals doing specific activities of interest. They are not conducive to the sharing for family reunions at their best.

Family Corporation Ownership

One unique example we are aware of that includes a lakeside cottage has worked well for friends of ours. It is a variation that could fit many other situations as well.

These friends had ancestors coming from Finland. They settled in Minnesota and built a cabin on a lake, complete with picnic area, old world sauna, etc.

Since the entire family learned to enjoy it, the property was transferred to the family in the form of a Family Corporation.

To work out an equitable arrangement, shares were established, granting access and privileges as well as requiring assessment and maintenance fees. Those living closer, who could and wanted more access, took more shares than those living farther away.

Arrangements were made to include support for stockholders who temporally needed relief from assessments and fees. This has worked well for several years. It is easy to visualize how this could work for other assets as well.

SMALL, INTIMATE MODEL

One in-law enjoyed our reunions and felt the need to establish a reunion with his side of the family. This started as a couple with four sons. During the past nineteen years this has become very successful in all aspects.

The sons have added wives, then children, until the group has grown to twenty-one. One of the third generation is now married and expecting a fourth-generation member to be added this season.

With the family scattered from North to South along the Eastern half of the US, they have chosen the Thanksgiving weekend as a traditional meeting date. This is the last of the long weekends that driving can be dependable weather wise. It gives them an opportunity to spend holiday time together.

They have chosen a centrally located State Park with the family taking a block of cabins that meets their needs. They pass the host responsibility, allowing the host family to use the cabin with a large central room that suffices for dining and meetings.

Each cabin has a kitchen that allows some food preparation. This, coupled with the baked goods brought from home, allows for everyone to experience, once again, the family favorites, the cook's specialties. By joining together, much sharing and bonding occurs year after year.

With this size group, a well established but less formal pattern has developed. With much time for working together, one-on-one exchange becomes easy.

Since they are an intense, athletic, competitive group, there is always outdoor games of volleyball and similar activities with some old, established traditions interspersed with new activities from time to time.

IMPORTANCE

OF PERSONAL SHARING

Perhaps the highlight of this reunion is the last afternoon when the group gathers in a circle for personal sharing.

As expressed before, there is no pressure to share beyond what an individual chooses. However, as the trust level grows, the desire to share with those who truly care about us grows with it. This has resulted in a level of knowledge, true concern, and understanding that most families can only hope for.

While some may feel this is intrusive, most of us, as years pass, appreciate this support. Few who reach senior status escape adversity. Whether it comes in the form of economic set back, health trauma, or premature death of a loved one, knowing that someone else truly cares is very comforting.

A VERY DIFFERENT
FAMILY BONDING

An unusual situation we are aware of involves a Texas couple with a large group of grandsons. Their focus is to develop these boys into well-rounded gentlemen.

Being from a ranching background and having a home on a large property, they used these assets. They built a "bunkhouse" and "game room" attached to their home.

Once each month they invite all grandsons—those from nine years of age and continuing until they are married or graduate from college, whichever comes first.

The focus of the weekend is fun activities coupled with the development of proper etiquette for a gentleman to get along smoothly in our present culture.

This involves some formal teaching, but mostly centers around the Saturday evening meal. Each month one of the older members is invited to come early with a younger assistant. The two of them work with the grandparents to plan the dinners. They then procure the food, do the preparation, serve, and host the meal—being minimally supervised as the grandparents feel necessary.

This hosting period is the most coveted responsibility of the program. This probably says much more about the warmth and nurturing abilities of the grandparents than about the grandsons.

It is easy to visualize the learning that takes place here:

- from the older to the younger Grandsons.

- from one grandson to a peer.

- from the Grandparents to Grandsons, in both formal and informal context.

This is, of course, an unusual situation, yet it illustrates what can be done with intentional planning for those who care.

THE STRANGEST EVER!

One Southern family meets annually with the women quilting and the men hunting squirrels together each day.

The evening centers on a different gourmet squirrel dinner each night. During long evenings of eating, bantering, and swapping stories, all stay in touch with the years' activities.

This may not be your or my choice…but, hey, if it works for them to accomplish their objectives, who's to disagree? I wish them many more years of this successful, close-knit family activity.

Keys to Secret Nine:

1) Consider several models.

2) Evaluate impact of special family activities on all members.

3) Recognize that effort and resources of special reunions will impact the future.

How to Keep
Reunions Ongoing

Secret Number Ten:
Keep in touch throughout the year.

> Always have a next great goal.
>
> Alan Kulwicki

Advice from "The First Lady":

Your success as a family...our success as a society...
depends not on what happens at the White House, but
on what happens inside your house.

Barbara Bush
~~~ from her commencement address to
Wellesley College Graduates, 1990

Your family is essential, your extended family is necessary,
and a family reunion can help you maintain those important relationships.

You know from prior chapters that I am a firm believer
in the intentional thought and planning that assures a successful reunion. Our experience at holding family reunions
has born this out.

However, I believe the success can be greatly enhanced by a series of contacts throughout the year.

There are many opportunities for keeping "up to date" with family, each taking varying degrees of effort and having varying effects and interest for different families.

The fit and effectiveness of these will depend upon the individual families. Much depends upon the proximity of family members, age of individuals, free time, schedules, etc.

OPPORTUNITIES FOR CONTACT

Don't miss the obvious. Holidays—such as Christmas, Memorial Day, July Fourth, Labor Day, and Thanksgiving— usually provide some extra non-work time that can be utilized for special visits or other contacts.

Also, the milestones in family life result in extra contacts and can be the best opportunities for intergenerational relationship building:

- Weddings

- Graduations

- Sporting events

- Similar celebrations

Obviously, vacation time can allow time to visit together or plan joint work projects.

Christmas with Siblings

It has been interesting to review the ways in which the Christmas holiday has helped us to build and maintain family ties.

As a family of nine growing up on a farm in Indiana, our early family ties were the result of parental influence.

Being a large, working class family in the 1920s and '30s, in our location, meant the major emphasis could best be directed to thoughtfulness, understanding, and celebration. Fortunately, our parents recognized the opportunity this provided.

We always had a Christmas tree, though usually very simple. Decorations were homemade. Strings of popcorn and "red haws" (fruit of wild hawthorn trees) gave a colorful effect on the green. We always celebrated the birth of Christ in the one-room rural home church. Most important for the family, however, was that all be present for Christmas day and any other significant event.

The first Christmas I vividly recall was 1935 or 1936 when I had my own money to buy each family member a gift. I had inherited from an older brother a weekly paper route with approximately twenty customers. The large paper, complete with magazine insert, sold for five cents per copy—with two cents per copy paid to the carrier.

I vividly recall giving one yard of gingham to my Mother (ten cents) for her to sew her own kitchen apron. One pair of supporters (nineteen cents) was given to my Dad that, on occasion, would hold up his socks on a Saturday afternoon trip to the County Seat or to Sunday morning church service. My family made me feel that I had been lavish with my generosity!

As the sixth child in the line-up of seven, I was the recipient of many lavish Christmas gifts of older siblings. They began to work away from home but always remembered. Often their locations were far from home, but home was ever in their minds.

Always the major emphasis was on all being together. No effort, by those remaining at home, was too much to honor those returning. Favorite foods, candies, cookies, and specialty items were planned and prepared weeks in advance.

It was only in later years that we came to realize what a wonderful gift we had received from this type of parenting.

CHRISTMAS AS PARENTS

With that family background and a wife who was an only child, the traditions and the influence of the larger family tended to dominate. Fortunately, our parents lived only thirty miles apart, so mutual visiting was possible.

As job assignments took us farther afield, parents visited us for Christmas on occasion. The help in assembling toys, baking, etc., was always welcome.

As our own three children grew in grammar school, we wanted to develop a thoughtful attitude in their lives. We elected to start the tradition that each family member would make (that is *physically make*) each other a Christmas gift.

The ideas and much assistance came from the parents, of course. Just imagine a family of five—three children, three years apart—each hand making four gifts per year. This adds up to twenty ideas to generate and construct each year. If you haven't tried it, don't underestimate the effort. After six or seven years, our idea banks and patience were exhausted.

Some of these gifts were duds! However, some were great, clever ideas and are still around with fond memories as the memories of late nights and frustrations dim.

No doubt, some will feel this is extreme; those who do may be right. However, it did build interest and thoughtfulness that has continued.

CHRISTMAS AS AN EXTENDED FAMILY

As individual families grew, the trips at Christmas time to the Farm became impractical.

For a while there was an exchange of gifts, by parcel post, to each member of each family.

Later, as the third generation grew and it became difficult to find appropriate gifts, it was jointly decided just to exchange a single "family gift." That lasted for several years; today many of our cherished vases, serving dishes, and practical items of daily use are wonderful mementos from that era.

Even later it was elected to make our "gift" a written document of each family's activity of the year to be mailed to the other six second-generation families in January.

We now have in our family archives some eight years of the interesting activities of the extended family.

As the natural cycle of life reduced the seven second-generation members to four and now to three members, we have chosen to use the more convenient communication technology of phone and e-mail for frequent contacts.

We visit together for a week in February largely to reminisce and share our experiences. Of course, we look forward to the family reunion later in the year.

Those accustomed to IM, e-mail, and blogs have many ways to keep in touch. Methods will change. Those with the desire to keep in contact will continually adapt and enhance the family relationship in the way that fits those best.

Group e-mail postings and protected family websites offer even simpler contact methods.

VACATIONS

It is natural that families with common interests and families of similar ages will be more inclined to vacation together.

This has been a source of great pleasure in some cases and does not seem to have generated problems.

Two second-generation families vacationed together on four wilderness trips, which included canoeing, backpacking, camping, fishing in mountain streams, and some visiting at one of the lake homes.

Several of the third generation visits each other's lake homes when conditions and time permits.

If a family is traveling in the area of another, a phone call, a meal together, or a brief visit is great if it seems convenient for all. If not, a phone contact is made and no one feels their plans *must* be interrupted.

On occasion an extended visit occurs, perhaps up to a week, of one family visiting another. Often this involves working together on a planned project or visiting some attractions of mutual interest with time for sharing allotted.

Of course, the word is passed quickly if there is sickness in a family. This results in calls, cards, letters, or other appropriate expressions of concern.

One Easily Overlooked Memory Trigger!

The mementos the host family gives to each family at the "dress-up dinner" was referred to in chapter five. This is a pleasant exchange that sometimes seems unnecessary.

However, it is an item that through the years adds to the memory of family ties. One second-generation sister has all of them, physically, in what she calls her "memory closet."

These are never expensive items. They are not meant to be; often they are handmade or assembled with care. These are around the house in various locations depending upon the usefulness or type of gift.

While all are valued as they are received, some seem to be kept and used in unpredictable ways. At the risk of offending, I will mention two that have a special place in our home.

One is a wooden heart, drilled to accept a candle stenciled "Families Are Forever." Another is a small olive-oil carafe that remains at our stove, used several times daily. Each time we see or use these items, we are reminded of the family who gave them.

No doubt, other families have mementos they notice more frequently than others. They are probably quite different from the ones that caught our attention. These are not more expensive or unusual, but for some unexplained reason, they remain in place after twelve years.

OUTSTANDING CONTACT ITEM: THE FAMILY DIRECTORY

This chapter has emphasized the need for and the many ways in which contacts through the year can enhance the interaction of families as well as contribute to the success of the family reunion.

We wandered into an outstanding idea of a booklet quite unexpectedly as we did many ideas that have become a part of the fabric of the activity.

It all started from the earliest days when, of necessity, a schedule was posted so all could assemble at the appointed time and place.

Next item to consider was the menu. When we were doing our own cooking and serving, a Duty Roster (Work Schedule) was also posted so assignments could be clarified. Most of all, everyone was happy to work but also happy to know when their responsibility ended.

Next, the family addresses and contact information was added. In today's world of street addresses, second homes, home phones, cell phones, e-mail addresses, etc., for most family members, we look forward to, and need, a new directory each year.

This has become a staple in the reunion planning and is relied upon heavily for contacts throughout the year.

It has morphed into a twenty-four page Family Directory and has become a necessary list of contacts, family history, pictures, unusual items of interest, and contact data. Where else can you go and find the birthdates, ages, and wedding anniversary dates of all family members, as well as family riddles, puzzles, old sayings (some called Daddisms), etc.?

Some of these are standard and expected by all. Some are one-time items that the host family decides. These are often historical items of interest, unique family facts, pictures, etc.

When done properly, this is a handbook of contacts for the entire family throughout the entire year. Since this has grown and become more complicated, software has been generated. This does much to simplify this laborious task. It is included in the Planning Toolkit referred to in the Resource Pages.

CONCLUSION

We are aware that we have been unusually blessed. We have avoided the difficulties we have seen in some families who go through periods of estrangement.

This is largely the result of the firm commitment of my mother and of the family being so firmly committed to being open, fair, and forgiving—also, our recognizing that none of us are perfect. Plus a strong understanding that love is not only a feeling, but also a decision.

Keeping in touch throughout the year and being thoughtful in as many ways as practical adds to the stability of the family.

This well-known adage, in practice, goes a long way. "Treat your friends like family and your family like friends."

ENJOY YOUR FAMILY

Enjoy those whom God has given you to accompany you on the journey of your life. Families are never perfect, and if you could ask my parents, they would tell you that families are full of challenges and aggravations. But you know what? The people with whom we share childhood memories, DNA, and a last name are a real blessing. You are on the ride of a lifetime.

T.D. Jakes
From: "Follow the Star" by T.D. JAKES
(available from www.successfulfamilyreunions.org.)

Keys to Secret Number Ten

1)   Build strong bonds in the nuclear family.

2)   Use each milestone for relationship building.

3)   Develop a significant and meaningful family directory.

Make Your Next Family
Reunion Fabulous
The Easy Way!

By reading *Secrets of Successful Family Reunions*, you have proven that you care about your family. Now you must show *your family* how much you care. Uncle Bob can help you. Bring your family together in a powerful, exciting family reunion.

Assure that your reunion will be the best ever by using your two *free gifts* and the *Reunion Planning Toolkit*. Your family will appreciate the fact that you have planned a great reunion and *made the gathering memorable*.

The youth in your family will have a great time. The family will renew their bonding and become better acquainted with each other. Everyone will appreciate the heritage they share, the history of their ancestors, and the values that have contributed to their lives. Also, they will have the opportunity to pass *their* legacy on to their descendents.

The teenagers are the hardest to keep interested. They can't stand boredom! They are also the ones that hold the key to the future of the family reunion. If they drop out, the cycle is broken. Hear what Megan Phillips, Lapeer, Michigan, one of our younger-generation members has said:

I've been going to the Wolfe family reunion since I was born; I am now twenty-two. I have so many wonderful memories from our family reunions. It's truly my favorite weekend of the year…Uncle Bob really knows how to make the family reunions not only a success, but also a special time for all the family who attends.

This is so different from the words we often hear, "Our youth are just not interested." The first of your *free gifts* will explain and illustrate ways you can keep your kids wanting more. The second *free gift* will answer many of your questions about how to make the reunion attractive to all.

A universal response to *Secrets of Successful Family Reunions* has been, "Great! But it looks like a *lot* of work." We grew into this gradually, but we know that jumping into this all at once can seem difficult.

To help you, we have prepared a Reunion Planning Toolkit so that you can follow the suggestions we have made with much less effort. Besides, it will give you the benefit of our forty years of experience. The hard work is done. *These tools will make it easy.*

The Toolkit comes with an iron clad, no questions ask, 30-day, money back guarantee! *Special Bonus* for readers of this book: 200% of your cost of this book!

Just logon to **www.successfulfamilyreunions.org**. Identify yourself and confirm that you have read the book for immediate information. See next page for more details.

Special
200% Bonus
$33.98—for readers of this book

Discount with purchase of the Reunion Planning Toolkit
(not valid with other special offers)

Free Information:

I. Five Games—from *Secrets of Successful Family Reunions* with instructions and pictures to help you see how best to use them.
FREE

II. FAQs—frequently asked questions. While each family is different, there are many questions that apply to all. Uncle Bob's answers will help.
FREE

To receive these free gifts go to **www.successfulfamilyreunions.org** click on *Free Gifts*, and download this information immediately.

The Reunion Planning Toolkit

The tools and guidance you need to make your reunion work.

To claim your $33.98 bonus go to our website, click on Reunion Planning Toolkit.

I. *Secrets of Successful Family Reunions*
   by Robert W. Wolfe

   Book format: With margins and white space for making notes, keeping records, etc. Use this duplicate copy as a gift to a Planning Partner or an interested friend.

   Audio Book format: For ease of review, so you overlook nothing.

II. *Hungry Like a Wolfe* (family cookbook)
    513 recipes from thirteen states with many family-comfort foods.

III. *Guide to Reunion Preparation* (with templates)
     Family Directory: Three different examples for your reference.

     Directory Software: So you can perform the laborious task of creating your own family directory the easy way.

     Sample Letters: Five samples for the needed announcements and contacts.

     Sample Accounting Forms: Four forms to minimize your record keeping.

IV. *Guide to Food and Accommodations*

    Food: Our Family plan, general helps, ideas from forty years of experience.

Accommodations: General Recommendations plus contacts for every state and geographic area

V. *Guide for Programs and Activities*
Guide to Programs and Schedule: Instructions, pictures, and sketches, etc.

Sermon (manuscript):
"Give a Blessing; Be a Blessing" also

Sermon (Audio): Great example for Family Instruction

Quickest way to order is to go to
www.successfulfamilyreunions.org

Complete the information, and the material will be shipped to you. Allow three weeks for delivery.